Conversations with Blob

A Guide to Spiritual Living in a World Gone Mad

By Lana Penrose

BLUE GAIA® — WORLD PUBLISHERS —

Conversations with Blob
A Guide to Spiritual Living in a World Gone Mad

Published by Blue Gaia World Publishers®
80 Glen Tower Drive, Glen Waverley
Victoria, Australia 3150

Email: info@blueangelonline.com
Website: www.blueangelonline.com

Edited by Stephanie Finne and Marie DelBalso

Blue Gaia World Publishers® is a registered trademark
and imprint of the Blue Angel Publishing Group.

ISBN: 978-1-922573-15-5

Contents

Preface

'Where the heck did *that* come from?'

That's what some people asked after reading an early draft of this manuscript and nervously breaking eye contact with me. It's a fair question that's difficult to answer, though it may have had something to do with me lolling about in a hospital bed with appendicitis, semi-sedated and bored out of my brain.

On the first day of my hospitalisation, a friend from my former life in the music industry invited me to hang out with him and The Cure — one of my all-time favourite bands. My eyes all but fell out of my head, and after being discharged, I joined him, vocalist Robert Smith and the rest of the group for dinner. But that has nothing whatsoever to do with this book. I just wanted you to know that I met Robert Smith!

So, back to the hospital bed. There I was, staring at the walls—drugged up, a dull ache in my side, not yet acquainted with Robert

Smith—when the idea for this material came with such force that I nearly tumbled to the floor. It was one of those rare occasions where I felt compelled to jot down notes *immediately*.

I began scrawling note after note and continued to do so well past my recovery, utilising every spare moment, possibly spurred by a couple of throwaway lines from my last book, *The Happiness Quest*, in which I scribed:

> "Was living a life of mortality sold to me by an eager time-share blob of consciousness who'd shown me glorious pictures of planet Earth but failed to mention life's proximity to the gore movie *Saw*?"

And:

> "While enjoying meditative states, I began to experience bursts of insight that are hard to describe. It was as if ... I now had a sage pacing around inside my head."

I began to wonder whether the blob of consciousness and pacing sage could be one and the same — a wise, witty and warm fictitious character to whom I could pose life's greatest questions, such as:

> Who am I?
> Why am I here?
> Is there more to this measly existence than meets the eye?

What follows, therefore, is a combination of my imagination and, without doubt, the regurgitation of a ton of metaphysical literature I have devoured over the years, or, more specifically, over the past quarter of a century. These are the concepts that have resonated with me and hung about in my subconscious until I tilted my head at just the right angle, causing them to fall out at just the right time.

However, my greatest qualification for writing this stuff is being human. Trust me when I say that I have messed up royally in my time, but, like you, I have never stopped searching for meaning. I am yet to master the art of living or every concept that follows. I don't pretend to be a great orator, oracle or expert. But I do invite you to join me in approaching these ideas openly, for I have found them to be extraordinarily insightful. Working intimately with this content has honestly changed my life.

Also, given the berserk happenings on our planet today, it feels prudent to be sending out a reminder that we are not hopeless individuals in a world gone mad. We are resilient, wondrous and courageous souls with extraordinary potential, and there is so much more to us than we give ourselves credit for, including our capacity to extend *love*.

I therefore hope that *Conversations with Blob* will not only raise consciousness but contribute to the greater good of all.

This book isn't merely to be read, but to be *experienced*.

Lana Penrose

Chapter 1. **You**

Hello? Can anyone up there hear me?

If you can, which I sincerely doubt, I sit here as a mystified human being, twiddling my thumbs and posing one of life's most confounding questions:

Who am I? And what the heck am I doing on this crazy planet?

I expect my query to fall on deaf ears. It always does. Whenever I cry out to the Great Beyond, I get nothing—a big, fat zilch—and truth be told, I'm growing weary of trying to work everything out for myself. Continually scratching this bulbous weighty thing atop my neck is becoming a tad tiresome.

So if **anybody up there** can hear me, I'd like to know ... **who on Earth am I?**

Thank you in advance,
Confused Citizen of the World

Dear Confused Citizen of the World,

Holy guacamole! Is that really you? *No way!*

I can't tell you how *thrilled* I am that we have at last connected! Believe me, I have been trying to reach you as desperately as you have me for a very long time. We in the Great Beyond do our darnedest to converse with confused citizens of the world. Given your propensity for confusion, I've had my eye on you for quite some time!

I guess I should begin by introducing myself. I don't have a name as such—how embarrassing—but I am what you might call a blob of consciousness floating about in the ether just beyond your usual levels of perception. I know it is customary for humans to label everything, so feel free to call me whatever you like — Chauncey, Delilah, Derrick ... heck, you can even call me Blob for all I care.

Whichever you choose, know that I am extraordinarily wise and sage-like, if I do say so myself — a being of light tasked with the honour of evolving humankind. Given that I am about to be granted that opportunity, allow me a moment to bite my allegorical knuckle and stare up into the heavens to prevent an invisible tear from streaking down my non-existent cheek.

Now that *that's* out of the way, I will say from the get-go that you are free to take or leave what I have to say, and I won't be offended in the least. However, I must reiterate that my high levels of wisdom run the risk of blowing your mind, so strap on a helmet and hold on tight. You asked: Who am I? And I think the best way to kick things off is to advise you of who you are *not*.

You are *not* a feeble, stinky, pathetic creature—flatulent, with fluctuating emotions, a head full of eyes, unpredictable hair and a mouth full of teeth occasionally decorated with spinach—who forages through metaphorical dumpsters in a never-ending search for scraps of love in the hope that someday something—*something, for the love of God*—will sustain you for just that little bit longer. No. You are not

....

that. You are *definitely* not that.

Nor are you a tiny, terrified grub inching its way across an open field beneath a murder of crows. You are not a helpless victim of life.

You are not your job title. Your life is *way* beyond a series of obligations for you to fulfil. Though the external world may pull you in a thousand different directions and demand your attention like a screaming brat of a child, you will never say, 'Man, I totally nailed that Excel spreadsheet' when you reach the end of the line. You will instead be grateful that you focused on your spiritual evolution, which is the fundamental reason we have connected today.

Yes, things are what they are in that bills need to be paid, but you *can* move through your days with more than emails, texts, invoices, meetings, mortgages, Instagram, debits and credits on your mind. It is altogether possible to put your dramas in their rightful place and see through the illusion of your so-called reality.

I would also like to mention that, as slick as it is, you are not your body. It therefore might be helpful to consider your physical vehicle, like an avatar, inhabited by your spirit for the purpose of exploring the weird and wonderful possibilities of life.

So, you are not a helpless victim, your job or your body. You are none of these things. Rather, you are this ...

And I pause now for dramatic effect.

Are you ready?

You are an *incredible* entity pulsing with perpetual, enduring, white-hot *love*, which makes the idea of you scavenging through dumpsters for skerricks of what you already possess in abundance just plain laughable — so much so that I am miming the act of mopping up tears in between my hearty guffaws.

....

You are a jaw-droppingly wonderful being blind to your own godliness. So transcendent are you that right now, in this moment, there is no need for you to add or subtract anything to make you perfect. Really try to hear me on this. Your spirit is impeccable. You are flawless. You are pure, divine consciousness in human form. Anything contrary to this is pretty much … I almost swore. Let's just say *false* because it too begins with an *f*.

Further, you and the Source of All Things—as in the explosive, immeasurable energy from which you originate—are not separate. You did not enter the world after flapping your maker a goodbye wave and saying, 'I've just gotta go and live this life thingy, but I'll be back before you can say, "She smelt vaguely of cabbage".'

No. At your core is Source energy. It is *in* you. You brought it with you. It is present right now, and it always will be. In other words, Source is not an elusive, external force quietly swirling and undulating in a galaxy far, far away. It is right here, right now. *It* is part of *you*. *You* are part of *it*.

It is vital that you comprehend the magnitude of that statement and do your best to acknowledge your divine essence. I know that on some level, the idea makes you squirm. 'More sugar with your god complex, dear?' But on another level, you know exactly what I'm talking about. Part of you remembers the thrill of erupting from Source as a divine spark and enthusiastically taking human form. You might like to indulge that recollection now. I'll be right here filing my (non-existent) nails as you do, so please take your time.

While you're at it, you might like to dwell upon the fact that you are *immortal*. You will never cease to be. Your spirit will never die. That means nothing can hurt you in an enduring way, and nor can anything be taken away.

Are you with me so far? I am saying that you are divine and eternal. You are love personified. Your essence is dazzling. Source

....

energy, ecstasy and peace reside within you. You possess enormous potential and astounding resources. Any beliefs to the contrary are erroneous. Therefore, I highly recommend that you drop the helpless grub shtick and pick up the mighty mantle of who you really are!

Whoa, whoa, whoa!

What the Dickens is going on here? Is this for real or have I tripped over the edge and into the looking glass? **Are 'you' a voice inside my head?** **Are you me?** What's happening? You seem to be suggesting that I'm something I'm not.

Ah! She speaks! But, my darling, 'tis true. And to answer your questions: something awesome, yes, no, yes, yes, something awesome, and, again, something awesome. With respect to your final query, allow me to elaborate.

I am talking about who you really are. I am urging you to bask in the luxury of remembrance. I am reminding you that you are not riddled with wickedness. Yes, you have messed up from time to time — who hasn't? But please don't regard yourself as guilty and 'bad'. Where there is light of such blinding intensity, there can be no shadow. It is important to know—to explore with vigour and *really* know—that the bigger You is kind, loving and faultless, and you are in a position to experience this more as you dance through your days.

By indulging the truth that you are a commanding being of light, you will yield to a greater volition that allows you to push past the false constructs of who you think you are. By continually recognising your innate innocence, you will draw your divinity ever closer.

I therefore press the point. You are innocent. Your core essence is like that of a newborn baby. No matter how much resistance this stirs up, it is the absolute truth. You are pure. You are beautiful. You are love. I don't just *think* you're enchanting. I *know* so for a fact.

It is precisely for these reasons that we have connected today: so that I can remind you of your inherent perfection, of your remarkable curiosity, of your hair that occasionally falls into place just so.

So ... spectacular ... now ... you. Okay?

(I've got to be making this up.)

As we chat further, I will be urging you to recognise your grace more and more.

(Either that or I'm losing my mind!)

I will be helping you to generate greater compassion, joy and light. I will be reminding you to love and serve in any way you can. I will be prompting you to realise that any spiritual exuberance you can offer will aid not only you, but your planet, including those who are lost in ignorance at this time.

I will be helping you to feel the divinity in and around you. I will be continually reminding you of the energies at your disposal that will help you to more clearly see the glorious richness of which I speak.

I will be inspiring you to sink into your own tranquillity as often as you can, allowing pure consciousness to be the focal point of your existence to propel you forward. I will be urging you to strive for the heart of who you are. I will be prompting you to call to mind your boundlessness, potency and spiritual freedom. Once your awareness shines upon the real You, the truth will set you free — and, boy, what an occasion that will be!

The more we talk, the more I will be unveiling the trappings of your four-dimensional reality, which is why I've encouraged you to be aware of your wonder from the very start. By raising your consciousness, you are opening your mind to that which is far more exhilarating, substantial and *real* than what you believe to be real today.

Wow! That's a lot of stuff you're intending for me there, Voice-in-my-Head, and all on the assumption that **I'm not a tired and fallible human** that is horrified by the world!

Beautiful soul, if you could but realise that you are not who you think you are according to your everyday mind, then your perception would shift. As I said, you know deep down that you are divine, yet your ego does its best to keep this well hidden. It dominates your thoughts and deeds and keeps you from recognising your spiritual self, which we will be chatting more about later.

For now, I will simply say that if you were to exist beyond the fog of your illusory self and recognise the Source energy within you (that is, your unbreakable connection to All That Is) you would be impervious to the ego-driven, attention-grabbing irrelevancies that snuff out your luminosity. Your egotistical chatter would finally shut up. And you would be free!

That is why I will be humbly suggesting that you be mindful of the babble and mini-tantrums that go off in your brain as you embody the personality of a three-year-old hyped up on red cordial; the whiny voice in your head that continually complains about being mistreated; the fractured you that craves attention and feels compelled to act out.

I will be encouraging you to engage your inner silence, for if you invite in the stillness, greater calmness will prevail ... unless, of course, you would prefer to continue twerking around your kitchen to the tune of a relentless whine.

No offence, but that last option sounds slightly more appealing! I'm still **freaking out** over your sudden 'appearance' **(or my sudden onset of madness)**. But even so, **may I interject?** In relation to me complaining, **have you seen what's going on down here? Have you seen the greedy, the hateful and the terror-loving nut jobs?** More to the point, **have you seen how mediocre I can be?**

I welcome your every interjection, my love. I am open to all that you have to say. And in response: yes, yes, sort-of-yes and no. But thank you for helping me to illustrate my point. It is precisely this type of observation that prevents you from bursting with euphoria. It is your self-judgement and failure to recognise the goodness in others that keeps you from experiencing the truth. I will be expanding on this a lot more in due course.

But to bring us back to who you really are, and following on from your flippant comment in relation to your own mediocrity, it pains me to hear a being of your grandeur turning on yourself in this way. You are anything but 'mediocre' as I have been trying to assure you since our conversation began. You have already achieved a great deal and evolved in more ways than you can count. Yet, despite your accomplishments, you focus on your failings. Should you err in any area of your life, you write yourself off completely. The judge within deems you hopeless, and from a tiny tincture of setback, you create a vat of failure from which you wholeheartedly sup. That's simply not on!

What's worse is the variety of façades you have erected so that you may present yourself in certain ways. Sadly, you have become as diligent at hiding your 'dark side' from the world as your 'light side' because—in relation to your dark side—if anybody knew what you were *really* like, they'd avoid you like the plague, and—in relation to your light side—it has become enormously uncool, if not obsolete, to showcase your spiritual inclinations in the ever-growing density of today's day and age.

But no matter how much you try to hide your dark and light sides, or how much you believe yourself to be a tiny, wretched monster or a 'weirdo' because you sense there's more to life than keeping up with the Kardashians, you will come to see that such self-concepts are not only unfounded, but of little use to anyone. Why? Because you are immortal, innocent, light-filled, unlimited and the personification of love. Everything else, all those odious images of yourself, are about as real as shadow puppets being projected onto a wall.

But I don't feel anything like the rapturous being that you're describing!

You don't? Well, it is my job to ensure that you do! And you will. Each time I remind you of a truth, another façade will be challenged and your vibration will heighten. In the interim, really try to hear me when I say that you are not who you think you are. It is *you* who judges and identifies with your false self. It is *you* who picks and chooses aspects of yourself and prods them forward like a pushy stage mother. It is *you* who manufactures your image. If you disentangle your ego from the equation, you would see that you are *perfect*. You would see that you are in a position to produce the performance of a lifetime. And you would see that you are *powerful*.

That sounds very hopeful, but is **there another way of discerning who I am aside from taking the word of a disembodied voice?**

For shizzle there is, Precious. By repeatedly asking 'Who am I?' — just as you did today!

You did something super-awesome by posing your Derek Zoolander question before. Through doing so, you took a step closer to knowing thyself. I therefore recommend that you keep asking — who are you, who-who, who-who ... 'cause you really wanna know! Trust me. You do! The answer is a brilliant one that far exceeds your current self-perception.

So, the next time you find yourself getting ticked off, ask, *'Who* is getting ticked off?' The next time you find yourself freaking out, ask, *'Who* is freaking out?' The next time you find yourself wolfing down a block of chocolate, ask, *'Who* is wolfing down the chocolate?' Who or *what* is behind the personality that you think you know so well? If you repeatedly ask, you will slowly come to recognise that there is an almighty energy that is 'living' you.

Why not start now? Dwell upon the perennial question and see if any revelations arise. Sure the logical brain might not come up with an answer and your eventual 'knowing' may come by way of a sensory response that will be, quite frankly, enlightening, but keep turning your awareness inward to allow the answers to fizzle to the surface like effervescent bubbles in a glass of champagne. Drop into the glorious space within, from which all knowledge rises.

The only thing standing between you and a lightning-bolt

....

answer is the notion that you don't already know who you are. In truth, you do. You, with a capital *Y*, is already aware. You, with a capital *Y*, is already switched on. Therefore, what you have been trying to discern for most of your life is right here, right now. It is present. It is *divine.* It is *you*. You *are* light, not *becoming* light in the far distant future.

You are on the brink of truly seeing for the first time in your life, of at last opening your eyes to your truth and that of everyone else. Never give up on your quest to awaken, and never allow the banality of everyday life to suck the drive out of you. Never allow anything to lure you away from what truly matters.

When being acquainted with the real You becomes your focus, when you systematically set that as your goal every day, you are building your energy into a crescendo that is destined to expand into a symphony of colour and light. Through curiosity, determination and practice, this will surely come to pass. And I, for one, cannot wait!

Okay, so you've got my attention.
In summary, then, **what does it all mean?**

My darling, it means that you are love. You are luminous. You are unlimited. You are immense. You are inherently serene, ecstatic and peaceful. It is time to zoom out from the image of the little you to reveal the big You. It is time for the truth to dawn, surpassing the most awe-inspiring sunrise that you have ever seen.

Everything that we have touched on today has brought you one step closer to remembering who you are. You are on course to transcending limitation and forfeiting your limited self-concept. And I am here to help you.

Source and all of us in the Great Beyond are at your disposal, full of hope, love, respect, reverence and deep admiration for your outright bravery to tackle an incarnation on the weird and wacky planet that you call Earth.

Till next time, Dear One, rock on! We salute you.

Exercise: Who are you?

As you sit quietly in your energy, pose the question:

Who am I?

Are you your job title? Are you a tiny earthling reading this book? Are you your limbs, fingers, torso, head and toes? Are you your thoughts? Are you your feelings? Keep asking:

Who am I?

And when it feels right, slowly zoom out and allow a wider perspective to begin to take form. Remind yourself that:

You are a powerful, wondrous, limitless being. You are love and light. You are an intricate and essential fragment of the vastness. You are an orchestra of melody, colour and movement that is nothing short of spectacular.

You are so much more than you think you are.

Sit with this for a while.

Feel the deliciousness as your connection to your true Self becomes so apparent that it warms your entire being.

Remind yourself that any self-image less than this is illusory. Yes, you are a living individual having a human experience with a head full of eyes, nostrils and teeth, but you are not limited by that or your current perception of who you think yourself to be.

For you are divine.

Cheat Sheet: You

- You are love personified.
- You are immortal.
- You are light.
- You are resourceful.
- You are innocent.
- You are peaceful.
- You are inextricably connected to Source.
- You are not a feeble victim of life.
- You are not your job.
- You are not your body.
- You are not your ego.
- You are not your judgement.
- Live in the moment.
- Ask for help.
- Your spirit is impeccable.
- You were born to love.

Chapter 2. **Why?**

Dear, um, Blob,

Given that you provided a selection of names to choose from, I think I'll go with that one for the simple reason that I find it the most amusing. But I have to say that I can't believe this is happening. **I'm astounded! Humbled! No, SPINNING OUT!**

If I seemed rude at the start of this about never hearing back from the Great Beyond, I'm sorry. It's just that I didn't expect an answer, let alone one so profound. Suddenly there you are sharing your wisdom as though we've known each other forever!

Now I'm scrambling to ask you something else for fear of you fading away. So, I guess what I'd next like to know is ...

Why am I here? That's right — only THE biggest

question posed by humans since the beginning of time! What am I supposed to be doing on this berserk planet? For the most part, I see my life as a chore. **What's the point?**

Can you shed any light? Are you still there? Blob? BLOB?
Yours,
Flabbergasted-yet-Anticipatory Human

Dear Flabbergasted-yet-Anticipatory Human,

Of course, I'm still here! I always have been and always will be, so don't expect to shake me off any time soon. We go way back, you and me, which is why our connection is so strong and one of my greatest thrills — and that's coming from an entity that is perpetually chuckling, floating and raising consciousness with its fellow blobby friends. I totally rate you!

....

Thank you for sticking around after I plunged into the big, heavy stuff right off the bat. It was a gamble, I know, but it paid dividends. And rather than you checking into a psychiatric ward, you are back for more and posing *the* perfect follow-up question, which is *so* you. I knew this would be fun!

So, why are you there?

I know you well, precious one. I know that you've spent a huge chunk of time not only posing this particular brain teaser but also eagerly anticipating the end of your earthly existence, not because you're a Cure-loving goth with a macabre death wish as such, but because you want to hurry up, get to heaven, chill out with the angels and be free of all the people, chaos, greed, need, injustice, sickness, celebrities, sleaze, insanity, media, corruption, terrorism, cruelty, violence, bitterness and fear. You wonder why you've been thrown in amongst it all. You find it monumentally confusing, and I understand why. I truly do.

Therefore, I will drill down the meaning of life into one comprehensive sentence to help ease your confusion:

> *You chose to be born into your world to love, evolve and serve your fellow people.*

That's why you find yourself grooving and shaking. *That's* the whole point!

If that doesn't sound sexy enough for you, rest assured that I'm not suggesting you drop everything and relocate to a developing country to feed the poor, although if you are that way inclined, by all means, knock yourself out.

However, I *am* suggesting that you love, respect and honour the divinity of every person you encounter—be it on the sidewalk, at the pub, at the supermarket, at work or on the bus—knowing that each individual has likewise incarnated to experience the uniqueness of being human.

Now, it didn't pass my notice that your eyes glazed over when I mentioned serving your fellow humans, so I should like to clarify. Service can be as simple as lifting your consciousness so that those around you unconsciously lift theirs as well.

You are awakening, my lovely. And you are in a position to *help*. I don't ask you to do much, but I do urge you to seize life's opportunity to get in touch with your inner self, your luminousness and your unconditional love — if not for your sake, then for the many who need you.

The media constantly focuses on that which is bleak. You watch on helplessly, viewing what appears to be civilised society disintegrating into a virtual dystopia. Hear me when I say, then, that the stuff we are sharing is more than a tad important.

Your fellow humans *need* you. Your fellow humans *need* your love. The world *needs* your service. The world *needs* you to keep trying. The world *needs* you to recognise your own worth and reflect it outward so that others may recognise theirs too. The world *needs* you to be a loving individual who is genuinely plugged into your pure, divine consciousness. This brings us to an extrapolation of my one-sentence answer to your gargantuan question, which was?

Why am I here?

Correct! Thank you. I was just checking to ensure that you were still awake!

You are a spiritual being having a human experience. You are where you are—incarnate on planet Earth—to remember your sacredness; to remember that you are divine; to love unconditionally;

to learn and teach; to heighten your awareness; to respect your body as it too is an expression of divinity and not just a meat suit you drag around with you. Your role is to reach upward and work with whatever is before you with the most expanded consciousness you can.

To arrive at this point of celebrating your divine, loving nature, of sharing your beauty and holding a mirror up so that others may see theirs too, is to live on purpose. This is true whether you are a bus driver, an aura cleanser or a production-line worker placing ball bearings into handheld fans to ensure effective propeller rotation. It is up to *you* to radiate your light dynamically and boldly in whatever situation you find yourself, both internally and externally.

To embody this knowledge is to truly know yourself. Any attempt you make to grasp what I mean by this is your ego's loss and the world's gain. So, keep searching for, feeling and sharing the light to usher in greater freedom for you and the planet. I will have more to say about this, but I'm watching your thought bubble expand as I speak. I therefore humbly await your next question.

Good Lord! You can read my mind? But, yes, my thoughts did start to wander when you mentioned production-line hand-held fans! I **was becoming secretly annoyed with myself for complaining about my life when there are so many people who are less fortunate than me**. I'm not really sure what I'm trying to say here ...

Oh, okay. Let me help you out then.

Your thoughts were gravitating toward the idea that the world makes even less sense when you consider those suffering not only on other continents but in your own backyard. Of course, you've been through your fair share of stuff, but when you consider hard-core abuse, addiction, poverty and illness suffered by others, it seems plain unfair.

Even though you've had occasion to find your own life arduous, you wonder why you've been born into a relatively fortuitous existence. You feel guilty for labouring through life and wasting time over comparatively insignificant occurrences. You wonder why you should be living such a 'charmed life' (that you loathe) while others endure genuine horror. You feel bad for being so 'lucky' — even though you forget just how lucky you are. And that's just the tip of the guilt-berg!

Am I right in thinking that my thinking has aligned with your thinking?

I couldn't have put it better myself!

But of course. That is because we are one.

Okay, let us now take a breath and break things down a little.

When musings like these come up, first use them as an opportunity to practise gratitude — not in a 'Tonight thank God it's them instead of you'[1] kind of way, but in a 'Thank you for the incredible opportunity that this life affords me' way.

Second, know that being born into a life of 'relative ease' comes with a certain amount of responsibility. You are less in survival mode, meaning you are in a wonderful position to work on yourself, learn, evolve, love and serve. Having a life like yours means there is less reason for you *not* to infuse yourself with light and shine brightly into a world that is, quite frankly, starving for illumination as much as those starving for food.

---

[1]   Do They Know It's Christmas ~ Band Aid ~ 1984
....

But the people we're talking about — the disenfranchised and such. Are they the ones that I'm meant to serve?

Yes and no. No, because who you serve is entirely up to you. You can serve the disenfranchised as much as you can the enfranchised! It is more about extending love and kindness to whomever is before you, regardless of their circumstances. You can love your family. You can love the homeless guy. You can love the falconry enthusiast. The goal is just to love.

The number-one question you will ask yourself when you shed your mortal coil is, 'How well did I love and serve others?' So, if you chose to serve in a soup kitchen, great. If you chose to serve as you exchanged toilet paper over a cubicle wall, also great!

The next time you catch yourself despairing over the state of the world and begin to drift into how horribly unjust everything is and start to feel jaded, angry, sad, guilty or whatever ... *stop*. Instead, remember that it is up to *you* to generate as much love, compassion and light as you can flood into the world. Focus on what is before you.

Again, loving and serving are *the* most important things you will ever do during this incarnation. To serve is to love. To love is to serve. They count, and any opportunity that allows you to exercise them offers a great clue as to why you chose to experience your earthly existence.

I guess I will try to love and serve as much as I can, then. Meanwhile, I hope you don't take this the wrong way, but **am I allowed to have fun while I'm at it?** This is all sounding a bit serious.

You are fantastic, sweetheart, so much so that if I had teeth, I would nibble you!

Yes, you are 'allowed' to have fun! You haven't been banished to your planet because you have been cosmically naughty and deserve to be punished. To love and serve doesn't mean donning a nun's habit or living a tedious life. You have every right to revel in your time on Earth, to have a blast, prance about and enjoy yourself. You are allowed to have a rocking, exciting, creative and happy time. You are allowed to be imaginative, inspired and vibrant, and to feel universal energy coursing through you. You are allowed to have moments of awe where your breath is stolen.

But believe it or not, these feelings can be elicited through loving and serving. 'Fun' isn't all about carnival rides and barrels of wine. To give *of* yourself is to give *to* yourself. The gift is in the giving. Therefore, regard serving as an opportunity, not a penance. The same goes for life. The nursery rhyme that suggests 'life is but a dream' is truer than you think. So be excited! This is *your* dream. This is *your* show that you get to direct, produce and star. The opportunities to demonstrate your loving nature are endless.

We will discuss this in greater depth as things unfold, but for now, I shall pause, for I sense your desire to interject again. Something I have said has made you feel weird. Don't ask me how I know, I just do, for I am Blob, and I know, well, pretty much everything. Plus, I just so happen to be floating about inside your head.

BRB — whenever you're ready.

....

Exercise: Why are you here?

Take a seat and have a breather. Give yourself permission to feel humble and harmless while reconnecting with the might and light inside you. Recognise that you—the real You, the bigger you, the spiritual you—is always, always, *always* ready to shine and share its light-filled nature with everyone around you. That aspect of your being has never faltered and never will. So with that in mind, gently begin to ask yourself:

> *Why am I here?*
> *What did I come here to do?*
> *What is the point of this life?'*

Sit quietly and go deeper. As you do, you may begin to hear answers from the bigger You. You may begin to hear whispers along the lines of:

> *You were born to learn and grow.*
> *You were born to look out for others, even in subtle ways.*
> *You were born to love and be loved.*
> *You were born to share love and light.*
> *You matter in ways most profound.*

You may *hear* nothing but *sense* something. Or, you may hear and sense nothing at all! But the more you quieten your mind, the more the truth will light the way.

Now, reflect upon the wonder of your spirit. It is present and alive right now on planet Earth. You are doing your thing, and what you are doing is already brilliant. You are always on course. You are a miracle.

....

Again, the more you evoke ideas like these, the more your spirit will awaken, which will open up more opportunities that allow you to love and serve.

Cheat Sheet: Why?

- You are here to be you.
- You are here to love, respect and honour the divinity of every person you meet.
- You are here to show gratitude.
- You are here to tap into your own luminescence.
- You are here to have fun.
- You are here to have a rocking, exciting, creative and happy life.
- You are here to be imaginative, inspired and vibrant.
- You are here to feel universal energy coursing through you.
- You are here to awaken.
- You are fulfilling your destiny.
- You were born to love, serve and evolve.
- You were born to learn, teach and heighten your awareness.
- You were born to respect yourself, your body and others.
- You were born to flood light into the world.
- You were born to give *of* yourself, which is to give *to* yourself.
- You are a spiritual being having a human experience.
- You were born to love.

Chapter 3. **Them**

OMG, Blob!

It really does feel like you're floating about inside my head. I'm tempted to say, 'Get outta there', **but I don't want you to leave**!

I didn't mean to interrupt you just now, but I was indeed itching to ask you another question, and herein lies my quandary:

You suggested that **my purpose is to love and serve others**, which is all well and good. But as hard as this is to admit, I have a **bit of a problem** when it comes to my fellow human beings. They scare me. They can be unpredictable, harsh and mean. They seem so different to who I am that trying to serve humanity will be no mean feat for someone like me.

What am I supposed to do? **How can I love and accept others when I'm scared of people?**

Yours truly,

Human-Being-Guarded

P.S. I feel awful asking that, but I sense with you, I can be frank.

Dear Frank,

Ah, yes. The old 'I hate people' thingy. I almost forgot about that!

It became more than apparent that others scared you when you first donned your Dead Kennedys 'I Hate People' T-shirt all those years ago, which I, for one, found utterly hilarious, albeit misguided.

However, if your fellow Homo sapiens continue to frighten you decades later, we certainly have work to do. Unfortunately, you do tend to be cautious around others in an effort to avoid being wounded, which creates the ideal circumstances for being wounded, if that makes any sense.

So, let us get back to basics. You incarnated into human form to get amongst it and experience the strangeness of being an alleged separate entity negotiating a virtual reality while attempting to shake off spiritual amnesia. It is a highly skilled game you're playing, and you entered it by choice because you really, *really* wanted to master it at a very deep level. It's like you're in *The Matrix* playing Neo, and situations and people keep popping up that aren't always to your liking.

But every dodgy and uncomfortable situation that arises occurs to help you to evolve and reflect upon what you're inclined to avoid. And, that includes challenging people. Your wariness of others is steeped in fear and judgement. Therefore, if you catch yourself fearing or judging, it indicates that it's time to check out what's really going on for you, namely, what is it about *you* that feels the need to either run or place yourself above *them*?

When you judge others, it can be a case of metaphorically stomping on your contemporaries' heads to feel bigger, better, safer or higher. You can be guilty of exercising self-righteousness when you'd be wiser to extend compassion. I say that because judgement is of no use to anyone. It is a tool used by the ego to keep you looking 'out there' or down your nose instead of within. It binds negativity to you.

Conversely, compassion does not. Compassion is an impeccable approach that fills you with goodwill and positivity, which you can then set free as though you are a toga-adorned goddess freeing a flock of white doves.

When people act in baffling ways, it can be helpful to remember that the being you are judging doesn't have the capacity to act differently at that particular point in time pursuant to their

....

circumstances or state of development. Everything others have been through—their upbringing, abuse, pain and/or environment—contributes to how they behave. Hurt people *hurt* people. Walk a mile in their shoes, and you'd likely act the same. And no matter how 'right' you think you are, others can always find imperfections in you, too ... if they look hard enough [*cough*].

You are all at different stages of evolution on your planet. Some of you have chosen to play particular roles out of curiosity, but generally, you've got wise old souls, inquisitive souls and nippy young souls all mushed up together. The latter is perhaps more prone to bite someone's ankle without apparent provocation, which, of course, can be more than a bit bewildering.

However, as improbable as it sounds, it isn't your place to judge anybody. You are all doing your best to evolve, and you were once young, too, if you'd care to cast your mind back. So, rather than maintaining a stringent focus on the confounding actions of others, you'd be wiser to turn your attention within and do all you can to *love and understand yourself* and *love and serve others* rather than focusing on your contemporaries' shortcomings.

That all sounds, ah, 'nice', Blob. But let's say someone does something abhorrent, like harm a child. What am I supposed to do with that? **There are things that people do down here that are plain unacceptable**.

Granted, that is a tough one, and I understand where you are coming from. Let us go back a few paces.

Thankfully, there have been points in your life where compassion has prevailed — over the misfortune of others, the plight of the orangutan, the tiger, the displaced; or toward those who have purchased products endorsed by celebrities in the hope of emulating their wealth, scent or gleaming white teeth. You clearly possess the ability to be compassionate!

So, whenever the opportunity presents itself—whatever that opportunity may be and no matter the magnitude—*generate compassion.* The more you do, the more easily accessible it will be. And the more accessible it is, the easier it will be to share it with those who have been victimised *and those who have perpetrated victimisation because the backgrounds of perpetrators are often the most painful of all.*

Compassion extends beyond reason. It allows light to enter the darkness. It moves beyond narrow perceptions and twists around bends to shine understanding upon complex situations. When you ace the art of being a loving, spiritual entity having a human experience, you will more easily offer empathy to whomever floats past your eyes and through your thoughts.

I know the idea of offering love and compassion to someone who has wounded a child or attacked your family doesn't sound very appealing, but baby steps, Dear One, baby steps. I admit, there *are* times when human behaviour seems beyond comprehension and forgiveness seems impossible. But when you awaken, you will look back and realise that there was never a need to fear, judge or so heavily invest in what is essentially illusion.

I realise this is a bitter pill for a human being to swallow, but once you reach Neo status (the part near the end where he recognises that he is 'The One' and there is no longer a need to fight), you will see what I mean. Till then, keep engaging your compassion and higher nature as you cultivate forgiveness and fearlessness. The more forgiving and fearless you are, the less inclined you will be to judge or wish ill upon anybody.

....

Well, I guess I'll need to shelve that one for now as it's slightly beyond my reach. Meanwhile, **let's say I frolic out into the world and find myself uncomfortable around people** — just ordinary, everyday people. **What am I supposed to do then?**

I suggest that every time you engage with somebody—a stranger, partner, friend or child—remember that *you help to create who that person thinks they are.* Feel the weight of that little nugget! Experience the thrill of it! You get to decide who the person before you is, how you will react to them and how that will make them feel. That means you are in a position to positively contribute to the person before you as though you are an eccentric artist wielding a brush.

Sadly, your artistry has been a little lacklustre at times. There have been occasions where you have projected hangover judgements onto people, thus generating your own discomfort. But it need not always be this way. You can allow others to intuit their sweetness, goodness and splendour through your thoughts, words, actions and reactions. The cheapest yet greatest gift you can ever bestow on another is to remind them of their innate perfection. By doing so, you cultivate your good nature as well as theirs. You grow from the love you extend, and so do they. It's win-win!

Remember, every individual who crosses your path is either consciously or unconsciously hoping that you will remind them of their inherent excellence. You have the capacity to grant them that wish. Also, remember that one of the primary reasons you are where you are is to love those around you.

Whenever you mix with others, you either contribute to their feelings of inferiority and worthlessness or to their divine expression. This adds to the overall energy of the world. Whenever you are in the presence of others, you have the opportunity to heighten their belief in their lower or higher-selves. This equally applies to how you relate to yourself in any given moment.

I think I get what you mean. But **what do I do if a divine soul with spiritual amnesia is yakking away in my face, the conversation steeped in negativity and banality**, which happens **ALL ... THE ... TIME**?

My darling, I hear you. Conversation in your realm is often delivered with an undercurrent of negativity — a regurgitation of unhappy news, including dire world events that engender fear. Telegraphing others' misfortunes or gossip designed to vilify others is rife wherever you go.

When you find yourself in a conversation heading in that direction, you might like to be still, go within and engage the truth of who you all are. You don't have to reach for a megaphone and make a major announcement. Just silently override all fallacy with truth. You are in the company of a divine being. So, too, is the person you are in company with!

So, the next time you are chatting away with somebody, allow the kinder you to connect with them. Listen without judgement. Such moments offer an opportunity to create something sacred. They help you to identify the oneness of all things and move beyond separation. It is the false idea of separation that makes people seem distant and life hard. So, expand away, Dear One, for practice makes perfect.

OMG. You *so* make me laugh!

I concede that there are people who can seem difficult — the ones who press your buttons and break your connection to peace. Yes, it is hard to be mellow with people like that braying in your face, and you would prefer to enjoy easier relations for the simple reason that they are, well, easier!

But one way of responding to difficult personalities is to give them a little scope. Rather than entering avoidance-mode, slacken the reins on how you expect them to behave. Love and let be. Loosen control. Soften expectations. Be patient. Forgive. Accept. Acknowledge that their actions aren't in alignment with who they are spiritually.

Remember the adage that those most difficult to love are those who need love the most. And know that stormy relationships have their place, too. Complicated relationships can help push you beyond your ego, see past illusion, dig deeper and evolve. They can teach you to stand tall, set boundaries and love yourself. As confounding as it may sound, they can serve a purpose, so really try to hear me when I say:

Love uses every opportunity at its disposal to make itself known.

That includes difficult people and complicated situations.

Similar to the Japanese art of Kintsugi—where broken pottery is pieced together with gold to celebrate the breakage and ultimate restoration—so, too, can tricky relationships be viewed as fine works of art, or fine works of art-in-progress. They provide an opportunity to showcase your alchemy should you manage to pull things and/or

....

yourself back together if they have shattered.

Having said that, I know that it isn't always easy to see others' divinity when they're behaving abhorrently or are heavily invested in incomprehensible delusion, which returns us to your original question, which was?

How can I love and accept others when I'm scared of people?

Right.

It may also be useful to bear in mind that you can love human beings without necessarily loving everything that they do. However, your primary objective is to see into the truth of whoever stands before you, using compassion as your guide. Regardless of who these folks are, regardless of what they do or don't do, no matter how aware or unaware they seem, all individuals are divine sparks. They have as much right to be having a human experience as you do by virtue of having been born. Ultimately, you will come to understand this, even though right now it may feel like a stretch ... of the type that does in a hamstring!

I realise that some of what I have suggested might be difficult to accept, but whomever your ego deems *good* or *bad*, that person remains of Source. Everything comes from Source and everything returns to Source. Source is good, and everything that has come from it has done so for a reason, which includes everyone and everything, whether *you* or *they* know it. So, add that to your thoughts, fears, postulations, hypotheses, judgements, ruminations and problems the next time you find yourself uncomfortable around people. It just might help.

But to **love one another** is easier said than **done** when you turn on the news and learn that somebody has just freshly hacked off somebody's head!

Dear One, I know, I know.

I know that when this happens, you regard the world and its inhabitants as insane and less than you are. It makes you feel better and somehow safer to think that you are separate from those who have perpetrated such acts.

If you need a blatant example of separation in your world, look no further than terrorism, which is separation at its finest, as is war. 'We're right; they're wrong,' 'We're better; they're worse.' That way of thinking, no matter the scale, breeds superiority, contempt, hatred, fear and inequality, and on and on it will go until the primitive circuit is broken.

However, to scale things back to your everyday life, the more you regard the world as a nightmare and look down on others as sinister, unpredictable and frightening, the more you will encounter such people, identify shortcomings in yourself (and others), tread on others' necks to keep them (and yourself) stuck, and add your negativity to the collective unconscious, thus helping to perpetuate the cycle. Attempting to explain this is tricky business, so thankfully I have no need for lungs; otherwise, I would have just passed out!

At its core, though, it is fear and fear alone that makes people act in unloving ways. As a purveyor of unloving acts yourself, once you acknowledge that you are occasionally driven by emotional pain, and that pain is simply pain—that it comes and it goes; that it can eventually be healed if it is blanketed with love; that it can be turned around and even embraced—you will no longer exert unnecessary energy in attempting to avoid it in yourself and others. You will be less inclined to judge as you understand others' pain-driven motives. Approaching things from this point of view will make your life easier.

One of the most challenging concepts to comprehend as a human is that from the highest perspective there is, you have never wronged anybody, and nobody has ever wronged you.

Okay, I know what you're thinking ...

I bet you do, considering I almost had an aneurysm! **Try telling that to the victims of rape, murder, sexual abuse, terrorist bombings, school shootings** and on and on it goes.

I totally hear you, my friend. I totally do. But before you kill me with your thoughts, I am merely hinting that when you truly start to understand the subject matter of our chats—what it really means to love unconditionally and to recognise your true nature and that of others—you will not only grasp the depths of your own sweetness but that of humankind. If that isn't possible for you right now, that's fine. You are where you are, and I say that without judgement and with the deepest compassion ... because I love you so hard!

But the only way to operate in your world powerfully—in the true sense of the word—is to move through it *fearlessly* and without intending harm through your thoughts, words, deeds or actions, and without putting yourself above or below anybody. I am hoping you will make it your goal to live selflessly and lovingly, reserving your judgement and other ego states wherever possible. I pray that you will step back and see that nobody can ever really cause you harm—not in an everlasting way, anyway—and that people aren't as scary as they seem, for they are of Source. I pray that you will also come to realise that you cannot fully live in the light if you cast others in shadow.

....

**Well, that complicates matters considering I'm still at a loss!
How can I possibly love without reservation in this dangerous world?**

Little deva, start by trusting *yourself*. You are a good person, and there are millions upon millions like you. Recognise the integrity and honesty that abounds, and charge your field and that of those around you with that energy as you do.

Remember that humans act cruelly when they are scared. Nobody acts fearfully unless they have unfinished business that can be resolved if they so choose. Every person in your world—whether they are aware of it or not—operates similarly to you: *seeking peace, love and happiness*. At the end of the day, it is what you all crave.

As you delve further into this work, you will begin to understand others and yourself more clearly. You will see beyond people's alleged flaws and façades and into the purity of those who stand before you. You will subtly remind others of their inherent goodness and therein lies service at its best, which brings us full circle.

No judgement. No fear. Just love.

Peace out.

Exercise: How can you love and accept others?

I would like to bequeath you this visualisation exercise.

Close your eyes, take three deep breaths and allow yourself the luxury of a moment's reprieve.

Once you have settled down, imagine you are wearing a thick, heavy veil. As you attempt to peer through your veil, notice how difficult it is to see. Notice that you can only perceive things in a distorted way. More importantly, realise that the veil does not allow you to see others for who they really are. It causes you to misperceive everything around you, to bump into things and register your world as shadowy and grey.

Now, take another deep breath and begin to lift your veil slowly. Imagine light and clarity flooding the scene. Start to see everybody in crisp, clear colour, as if for the first time. See the dazzling brilliance of each passer-by as they parade past, unaware of their own glory.

With your veil now lifted, imagine your judgements falling away. Imagine those judgements being replaced by compassion, and recognise that everyone is travelling their own unique path. Notice the keen, sharp picture that allows you to see into the heart of every being. Notice each perfect soul learning, growing and doing precisely what it has come here to do for the sake of universal evolution. And notice how radiant, perfect and lucky you are to be cast among such extraordinary company.

Feel yourself filling with awe. Remind yourself that everybody is consciously or unconsciously seeking peace, love and happiness, and that those most difficult to love are often those who need love most of all.

Sit with any sensations that arise, then slowly open your eyes. And ... scene!

....

This visualisation is best carried out in the morning with a view to taking it into your day to enjoy veil-free encounters. Try it today, then tomorrow, then the next day, until your improved perception becomes the new norm.

Remember that you will never experience the light if you cloak anybody in darkness, including yourself. And that seeing into the truth and interconnectedness of all things is to the world's advantage.

Cheat Sheet: Them

- Every being is a divine spark.
- Every being has purpose.
- Every person is a manifestation of Source.
- Every person is unconsciously hoping to be reminded of their inherent perfection.
- Every person is seeking peace, love and happiness.
- Every person is influenced by their own unique set of circumstances and evolution.
- Fear motivates people's negative actions.
- If you walked a mile in their shoes, you'd likely act as they do.
- Judgement is a tool used by the ego.
- Compassion is a tool used by the soul.
- The more you look down on others, the more disconnected you feel.
- People who are the most difficult to love are often those who need love the most.
- Hurt people *hurt* people.
- Love uses everything at its disposal to make itself known.
- You were born to love.

Chapter 4. **Ego**

Dear Blob,

Wow! This is really heady stuff. I'm still blown away by actually having heard from you, let alone the depth of our conversation. You do realise that I'm just an ordinary girl living an ordinary life, don't you, and I'm not the Dalai Lama, Mother Teresa or anyone of particular note? I'm tempted to ask 'Why me?' but I have a hunch you'll refer me back to chapter one, and we'll have to start all over again, so scrap that and know that I'm with you so far:

People = Good. Judgement = Bad.
Too easy [*cough*] (to borrow from your earlier quip)!

Now, let me throw a quick one at you based on something you said before. You mentioned 'ego' which to my mind has several different meanings. If people have big egos, it usually means that they're full of themselves. For Freudians, it means the part that mediates the conscious and unconscious minds ... or something. And when you say it, it's like it has another meaning altogether.

So, what do you mean by 'ego'?

(And do you agree with the Skyhooks' sentiment that 'ego is not a dirty word'?)

Glam rock forever!

Dear Glam Rocker,

Was that some kind of test to determine the breadth of my classic-rock knowledge? Throw an obscure musical reference my way, and I'll get it every time! Skyhooks was an Australian band formed in 1973, and the song in question peaked at number one in the

....

singles charts in 1975. However, while I *love* playing air guitar to that particular tune, I've never entirely agreed with its sentiments. Yes, in and of itself, ego is *not* a dirty word; it is simply a word. But ego in the context of our discourse isn't the part of you with which I recommend you align.

My definition of ego is the small you, as in the *you* with a little *y* as opposed to the real *You* with a capital *Y*, which is the bit that operates from a higher perspective that is beyond pettiness, judgement and unwarranted craziness. So, let us have a little chat with that definition in mind.

Sometimes you feel bad because your thoughts go from saintly to poisonous in the blink of an eye. They go up and down like a cartoon shark's jawline all day long. You judge and critique. You deem what's right and wrong. This commentary comes courtesy of your egoic mind, and indicates that you are identifying with the animal aspect of your human nature.

When your ego is in charge, it is impossible to keep your thoughts pure and kind because it simply cannot sustain that way of thinking. It isn't really interested in thinking in that way at any rate because it enjoys shooting daggers, then transitioning back to pious. Good thoughts, bad thoughts; approving, disapproving. That's just how it rolls.

I can sadly relate! So, let me ask you this: If my ego is unwilling to maintain a loving state, is it 'incurable'? **Am I doomed to be horrible forever?**

No, you are not! And *incurable* isn't really the right word.

Allow me to throw a metaphor your way to better illustrate things as I see them. Picture your ego as a rambunctious baboon and your soul as a sturdy tree. See the baboon clambering all over the tree. As our furry friend scrambles over boughs and branches, grunting and screeching, it doesn't miraculously take on the characteristics of the tree and become still and silent. Likewise, the tree doesn't take on the characteristics of the feisty baboon.

These two distinct ways of being are available to you. You can either choose to nurture your tree-like nature, and root yourself in remaining steady and serene, or act like a rowdy baboon. It's entirely up to you. But the more you tune into your tree-like self, the more you will calm down, flourish and be still. You will be less inclined to judge others who are acting like baboons, for you will accept their nature at that point in time, remembering the many times that you, too, have hurled bananas and other unmentionables, and jumped up and down baring your offensive behind!

When humans engage their baboon-like nature, they are usually operating from a primitive place of fear. This is often more apparent if you've been hurt and approach others with mild trepidation to self-preserve, which breeds a greater sense of separation. And that right there—that fear and separation—*is orchestrated by your ego.*

Broadly speaking, this is 'fight or flight' stuff, which, of course, is perfectly acceptable if you happen to be a primate ... *which you are not!* You are a spirit in the material world, as our good friend Sting once warbled. From a spiritual perspective, there is never a need to fight, and the only reason you would ever choose to fly would be for the joy of it!

So, in short, it is your ego that keeps you feeling afraid or stuck, and it is your inner-judge that keeps you feeling superior yet limited.

Are the 'ego' and 'judge' the same thing?

Indeed they are. I use those terms interchangeably, so well spotted!

You have surely noticed the monologue that takes place inside your head that adjudicates your every move and those of everyone around you. *You're* not good enough, *they're* not good enough, you need a bone reduction because your finger's too pointy — that type of thing.

If you examine your thoughts more closely, you'll see that the judge fires off non-stop criticism towards nearly everything it focuses on, particularly things it deems threatening. From the perspective of a separated being, that's fine — a warped means of keeping you 'safe', as counterproductive as that is. But, again, you are *not* separate from anyone. And you are *not* a primate. You are a spirit ... in the material world!

And given that you are a spirit in the material world, you are in a thankful position to identify with your true self whenever you set your mind to it. By constantly reminding yourself of your spiritual nature and that of everyone else, and by doing whatever it takes to *experience* that nature, you will be able to maintain higher thoughts. I will be dropping instructions on how to do this more as our dialogue unfolds.

In the meantime, by tuning into the truth of who you are and *living* that truth, you will be better able to offer love to *yourself* and *everyone* on a more consistent basis. When you become fearless and relinquish your ego, this will deepen. Approaching things fearlessly is one of our primary objectives, and fearlessness will come more into play when you act from your higher nature.

If you are able to sustain that way of being, you will connect with others from a place of warmth and safety. You will move freely through the world and interact without trepidation, rather than feeling restricted, spiky and like a monkey hopping on one leg and scratching its armpit.

But can I shut down the ego altogether? If it's behind all the torment I put myself and everyone through, **I'd like to be rid of it once and for all!**

Ah, Dear One. That's what we call enlightenment, and I will be sprinkling countless suggestions throughout this narrative to help get you there. Trust me when I say that there is a method to my madness in how I am repeating and dispensing this information to you. By stealthily bypassing your ego, I am planting seeds and heightening your vibration as we go without anybody (or 'it') particularly noticing. It has already begun.

Sorry to be impatient, but I'd prefer to be rid of it NOW!

Impatient? A human? *Never!*

Okay, here are a few more clues for She Who Cannot Wait.

Of course the ego will cough, splutter and protest over the prospect of being annihilated, and you can't really blame it. After all, it has gotten you to where you are now relatively intact. And to a degree, you need an ego to exist in your world. However, as one of my good friends once said, it is possible to be *in* the world but not *of* it.

So, rather than attempting to kill off your ego, I suggest you gently embrace your divine power, the goal being to fold the ego into the mix while keeping all your bits where they belong.

Your ego parts are allegedly there to ensure your self-preservation, but they must know their rightful place and heal into

. . . .

the whole. By surrendering to something bigger, they will less feel the need to yell so loudly, and you will begin to enjoy more serenity.

An analogy that might help you to comprehend what my invisible gums are flapping about is to imagine an inflatable dinghy with all of your ego aspects seated around it: your fearful self, angry self, nasty self, sad self and the rest. Imagine one of these characters abruptly standing to make itself known, which runs the risk of capsizing your vessel.

If all of your parts were to sit in their proper places with their life jackets on, and if they all had a voice but were disciplined enough to use them only as needed to keep you genuinely safe, your entire crew would remain steady, afloat and buoyed by your dinghy — where the latter represents your higher self.

Another way of looking at it—if you prefer land to sea—is to imagine your ego parts as passengers on a bus, the operative word being *passengers*. In this scenario, the bus driver is your higher self who is there to steer you in the right direction while your ego parts go along for the ride. It is preferable for them to stay in their seats and enjoy the scenery rather than clamber over the driver and veer you off course!

Does that make sense? I am saying that it isn't worth tussling with your ego to the point of qualifying for the WWE World Heavyweight Championship. Instead, observe your funny little ego friends as they go about their business of allegedly protecting you and doing their thing. See them flit here, there and everywhere, obsessing over X, which is a lot like Y, not really varying their routine after all these years, and—if you don't mind me saying—being quite boring, predictable and neurotic.

If you were to transcend this craziness, you would no longer be dominated by limited thought. You would feel more peaceful, content and safe while experiencing a heightened state of awareness. The more you exercise this, the more your ego will relax. Even *it* will come to realise that it is preferable to going around in circles until everyone throws up!

However, in terms of where you are now, you are fortunate to have an ego banging a wooden spoon against a saucepan because it provides the perfect contrast to where you soon will be. You will see serenity more clearly when it stands proudly before you. The more you exercise these concepts, the more your ego will relinquish its grip.

As you put our discussion into practice, you will be less inclined to muddle your way through life with a bunch of ego voices barking inside your head. The nasty you, the frightened you, the defensive you, the bitchy you, the cast of thousands that you carry around with you, are little more than phantoms that have been brought to life to misguidedly protect you. They need no longer dominate you in the way that they have. They have nothing whatsoever to do with your true self. Nothing at all. They are so far removed from who you really are that they are closer to spectres that aren't even real. Rather than keeping you protected, they keep you enslaved.

The excellent news is that it will soon be possible for you to see through your ego's façade and that of others, and into your shared divinity. The time will come where you will view each individual, including yourself, as a godly entity having an earthly experience rather than a god-awful entity having an ugly experience.

The aim is to keep your intentions high, maintain your purity and refrain from wishing ill upon anybody. God knows some of your thoughts have sprouted fangs and spat poison at times, so if all else fails—for now, at least—make like you are a non-judgemental, compassionate and inherently good being, if only for the fact that *you actually are*. If you keep acting in the way that you would prefer to be, self-correcting as you go, a more natural way of being will begin to take hold.

In any event, I sense that you have reached an understanding of what I mean by 'ego', so be excited, my lovely, for we are another step closer to getting you high.

Now, if you would be so kind as to excuse me, I must tend to a gentleman in China who is requesting my help. *Ziajian*, as they say in that neck of the woods. Or, as they say where you're from, I'll catch ya 'ron!

Exercise: How can you rein in your ego?

You, or rather your ego, are an amazing critic. Your ego offers a running commentary on your actions and those of your friends, bosses, colleagues, partner, family, police, drivers, commuters, shoppers, pedestrians, butchers, bakers, candlestick makers, filmmakers, baristas, bankers, fishmongers, teachers, politicians, telemarketers, celebrities, and on and on it goes.

Let us look at how you can become more aware of its shenanigans. This exercise is most effective if carried out regularly — until you at least begin to notice the nuances of your internal chatter.

Phase 1. Close your eyes, take three deep breaths and tune into your thoughts. Begin to recognise the never-ending babble and nonstop critique that prove you are viewing things through a distorted lens.

Phase 2. Observe your mind's machinations more closely. Note where your thoughts flit to. Note the subject matter. Note the repetition. Be aware of the self-talk, the judgement and the barriers that your ego industriously erects to keep you enslaved, recognising that it is grinding you into the ground and keeping you stuck where you don't want to be. As you do this, try not to judge yourself for being judgemental, for that will only re-establish the ego!

Phase 3. As your thoughts continue to race, call in your inner stillness. Become 'aware of your awareness'. Ask 'who is aware?' Feel your higher, lighter and kinder self extending beyond your egoic boundaries. Allow yourself to slip into a state that aligns more accurately with your true nature. Allow your consciousness to soar beyond the banality. Proclaim that you are no longer content to live a life disconnected from who you truly are and from whom everyone else is either.

Be still, for deep down you are free.

Cheat Sheet: Ego

- The ego dispenses judgement and criticism.
- The ego has nothing to do with your true self.
- The ego usually operates from a place of fear.
- The ego cannot sustain a loving state.
- You are a godly entity having an earthly experience.
- Identify with your spiritual, 'tree-like' self as opposed to your ego's 'baboon-like' nature.
- Introduce your inner silence to end the ego's neuroses.
- Invoke your spiritual side to sustain kinder thoughts.
- You are a spirit in the material world.
- You were born to love.

Chapter 5. **Source**

Dear Blob,

Thank you for clarifying who I am, who they are and what my ego is. That last one, for all intents and purposes, sounds like a royal pain in the butt, so let's move onto bigger and better things, like the Big Kahuna in the Sky.

Yup … I wanna know about God.

I realise that we're entering dangerous territory here, given that many squirm over this concept nowadays. Down here we've got nonbelievers, fundamentalists, fence-sitters — the whole kit and caboodle. But you've referred to 'Source' many times now, so I gather by that you mean God. So, tell me once and for all … **Is there a God?**

A loaded question for sure, which is **why I can't wait for your response!**

With warmest regards,

Wretched Inhabitant of Planet Earth

P.S. I hope my question has not caused offence.

Dear Perfect Inhabitant of Planet Earth,

No offence taken, for it is impossible to offend a pure blob of consciousness. We are way too advanced, impartial and immersed in perfection, plus we see you only as curious and sweet! Also, believe it or not, you are not the first person to have posed this particular question.

But the answer is *yes.*

Yes! Yes! A million times *yes!*

There is indeed a God.

Surprise!

....

I am hyper-aware that you and many others dislike what some term 'God-bothering', or being bombarded with dogmatic spiels, so, being mindful of this, I will be as concise as I can, which isn't easy given the enormity of our subject matter, which is God, for God's sake! But there is *absolutely* a God, whom I refer to as Source — a profound energy field from which all things originate and to which they will ultimately return.

You seem supremely confident about that.
Would you care to elaborate?

I surely would! If I had a throat, here's where I'd clear it.

Source is an infinite, dynamic force that is so exhilarating it makes me reel just thinking about it. It is so loving and benevolent that it almost makes me want to weep. Source is beatific. Source is ecstatic. Source is peaceful. Source is powerful. To experience Source is to experience pure joy.

Source energy is so potent that it fills every molecule of the multiverse and beyond. It creates and expands continuously, infinitely, relentlessly, inquisitively, perfectly and gracefully. It is hotly active, omniscient, gentle, tender and present at all times *for you*. It regards *you* as its most precious child, as though its very existence hinges upon you, for you are an expression of it, which makes you priceless by default.

Make no mistake: you were born of this incredible phenomenon, that which is endlessly warm, consoling, divine, loving and compassionate. It waits patiently for you and is available 24/7. Never forget that, and never forget that it *lives in you*! Take a moment to feel the weight of that statement. Source *lives in you*. It wants nothing more than for you to cosy up to that fact. It longs for you to experience its divine energy. It yearns for you to share in its exultation, euphoria, ecstasy and bliss.

It. Loves. You.

As in *really, really* loves you to a degree that is destined to blow your mind. Nothing—no love affair, drug, relationship, child, puppy or hamster—*nothing* comes close to experiencing the love of Source. Unlike many human relationships, Source loves you unconditionally and with all that it's got, which is *everything*. If Source had a tattoo bearing your name, it would never look back!

I therefore urge you to do all in your power to sense Source within you. I encourage you to tap into your heart centre where this energy dwells. Do this consistently and you won't look back either.

That sounds thrilling, Blob, and I don't mean to sound blasphemous, but if something that big and mighty **existed within me, then wouldn't I know it?**

The fact that you can't yet feel what we in the upper realms do would make me feel sad if I knew such an emotion. Instead, it fills me with elation because I know without a doubt that one day you will. Recognising the mightiness within you is inevitable, and with each turn of the page, you are getting closer.

The only reason you don't feel it right now is because your ego and preoccupation with the external world does not permit it. However, if you would like to experience more of what I speak, you could begin by saying something like, 'Source thrives in me now'—or however you'd like to phrase it—*then be still and sense it.*

I don't mean to be rude, but you seldom slow down enough to take notice of what is hiding in plain sight. And I don't mean to sound like a televangelist when I ask you to please re-read what I've just said, only this time with *feeling*. *Source thrives in you now*. It genuinely does. There is no separation between you and it. It *is* you, which is no more blasphemous than your question. As far as I'm concerned, anything to the contrary is closer to profane.

Now, these aren't merely words for you to breeze over as you race toward the finish line to check another book off your reading list. They're not for you to digest and discard, focusing on more pressing matters like who's hooking up with whom on reality TV. It's lovely to be all wistful, dreamy, thoughtful and theological when it comes to musing over whether or not there is a God, but thinking about it rather than *experiencing* it is about as enthralling as watching your leg hair grow.

Source is so much more than an idea, which is why I urge you to get stuck into *feeling* your inherent divinity *now*. The more you attune to it, the more your ego will relax.

So, again, I remind you that the Divine is alive in you. It's true! And it's *huge*. No, make that ginormous. But, hey, don't just take my word for it, or offhandedly dismiss it, or intellectually process it and move on. Don't put this book down and revert to feeling isolated and small. This is your absolute truth, so *own* it and *live* it by integrating it into your daily awareness and experiencing it as often as you can for the rest of your life.

Source thrives in your heart in this very second.

Okay, okay! I hear you. But I don't know if I believe you! Not as much as you'd like me to, anyway. If it's in me, of me, around me, or however else you'd like to put it, then **why haven't I felt God when I've needed to the most?**

Angel, during your times of despair—when you've spluttered and

....

64

cried and banged your head against the wall—divine energy has always been there for you because you are loved and treasured beyond your wildest imaginings. Your sound, colour, harmony, resonance and beauty are essential to the overall makeup of All That Is. You are deeply loved and respected by your creator because your creator deeply loves and respects itself. You have never been forsaken or overlooked, for that would be impossible. The Divine ignoring you is like staring into a mirror and trying to ignore your own face!

Unfortunately, your ego has blocked the flow of energy between you and Source during your times of despair. It has been more comfortable identifying with your dramas, which has been a travesty. You have therefore shrunk inward, lost in the effort of staving off your pain. Your grief has intensified. You have felt alone. The 'hearts' of a thousand blobs have broken on such occasions, when Source has attempted to console you but you have been unable to accept its sweet solace, when you have retreated from the immensity of your God-self and your own worth. But that's okay. We understood!

Now we would like *you* to understand! No matter how futile things seem, and whether you sense it or not, you are always offered comfort, for you are beyond precious. *You are always offered comfort by Source because you are divine. Your creator never abandons you. It does not wish pain for you.*

Through the eyes of Source, your life has deep, profound meaning, no matter how tragic, right or wrong things appear. You have a vital role to play. You are an integral and irreplaceable element that has been carefully woven into the fabric of the universe. Regardless of the situations you find yourself in, you are where you are meant to be for very valid reasons: to love and be loved; to heal and grow; to serve and be served. You are living a perfect and purposeful life. And you are loved beyond your wildest imaginings by the orchestrator of it all, simply for being you.

....

If you want to feel a deep, abiding connection to the loving energy that flows from the greatest force that exists, it is yours for the taking no matter what is going on in your life. You can access Source's intoxicating energy any place, any time, regardless of your circumstances.

Source is beyond eager to share itself with you, and you are invited to relish its security, knowing that the love of the Divine is part of you and always will be.

That sounds comforting, but **are we talking about the God of religions here?** If so, there are plenty to choose from, so which one is **'right'**?

A splendid question! And in many ways, they're *all* right!

I know that you aren't personally into the man-on-a-cloud stuff, despite your 'Big Kahuna' quip earlier. You are fairly confident that God is beyond growing a beard and has no need for a beard-trimmer. I can confirm that this is so!

I can also confirm that Source is not a punitive father figure who marks black crosses against your name when you mess up, which I hope brings you relief given that nobody likes an ink shortage! But I am saying that Source does not dispense more love to you if you do something 'right' or withhold love from you if you do something 'wrong'.

'But who is the real God?' I hear you croak with desperation. Well, Source is an unlimited energy *source*. The clue is in the name! Consider the power from which all things emanate. Consider the immensity of space expanding into infinity. That expansive energy is, in effect, what most religions call God, though it is symbolised in different forms.

....

The best way to comprehend what I am attempting to articulate is to wrap your *inner knowing* around it rather than your intellect, for the brain doesn't always compute. I realise that this isn't a walk in the park for you, considering we're discussing something intangible. But if it makes things easier, simply sit with the idea that you and the Divine are far more limitless than your current perception allows you to see. You are part of something vast and incomprehensible.

Rather than attempting to comprehend what God is logically, try immersing yourself in the *essence* of Source (which is more than an ambiguous menu item)! Imagine what it might feel like to experience something so mighty that it defies logic. Imagine being part of something so powerful, loving, indestructible, immortal, attentive, protective, wise and perfect that the most spectacular adjectives in every known language could never do it justice.

To immerse yourself in God, conceptually or otherwise, is a wonderful feeling. I am told that no earthly experience can compare. But, hey, what would I know? I only know that *Source is love*, and that its love for you is boundless, unlimited, consistent, unfathomable, unwavering and enduring. Its love for you is of such infinite magnitude that it's tricky to convey, as it is currently beyond your understanding pursuant to the morsels of love that you have tasted to date. But isn't that something? You are of *that!*

Wow. That really is something! But, like I said, I haven't felt anything remotely like it. **I'd like to experience it!**

Okay, well, let's try something now.

Ask yourself, 'Without altering a single thing in my life—that is, keeping every circumstance exactly as it is—how can I feel Source?' Think deeply about it by drawing inspiration from your soul rather than your brain.

If you do this, you will begin to experience Source energy simply by *deciding to experience it* and *by continually returning to that decision.* It is a *choice* to feel God. It is about fine-tuning your focus. Remember, Source is unlimited. It has a perpetual connection to your energy system that can never be broken. It is up to you to turn your attention to that connection rather than sitting there, twiddling your thumbs and wondering why you feel a bit wrong. *It is a choice.*

You live in a world populated by millions of jaded people, where the concept of God is either scoffed at, dismissed or used to wage wars; where powers beyond the five senses are the stuff of nonsense and considered make-believe. But I am here to tell you that *God is real* and you are doing yourself an enormous disservice by thinking otherwise.

By desiring to reconnect with Source you reignite vital energy that can be felt by others and improve your life, not to mention the world. Although people may have no conscious awareness of the spiritual gymnastics you are performing, your Sourced-up energy has the capacity to stir something in others that will subtly remind them of their own divine nature. By consciously embodying God, miracles will start to unfold by virtue of viewing life from an expanded perspective.

By tuning into Source and feeling that energy course through you, you will experience some seriously far-out stuff. By choosing to tune into a higher power, you will exude great energy regardless of what is happening around you, for you will be attuned to the greatest vibration there is.

Now, I am about to go even deeper here, so bear with me as I shimmy further into my metaphorical couch befitting of a highly respected orb of my stature. You might like to picture it as red, gold and velvety as I do in your head!

While absorbing these words, I have seen you switch on, and

what a glorious sight it has been to behold! Yet I have also sensed that you are bursting to reunite with Source 'one day', which indicates that you still believe in the fable of separation — that you are separate from Source; that you are a separate individual that has a long way to go before arriving at your destination; that you are separate from everything. In reality, you don't, and you aren't. You are *not* a solitary entity fumbling around blindfolded, aiming to hit upon God as though it were a piñata!

> *You are already 'there.'*
> *You are already blended with Source.*
> *Source is already in you.*

Dear One, I cannot help but reiterate this over and over, to prod you toward becoming more conscious of your connection. I know you're picturing me waving my hands in the air and falling one step short of proclaiming, 'Hallelujah, brother!' but again I ask you to *feel* what I'm saying. Really do your best to remain switched on and sense the magic fusing between you and Source, for courting this energy can be hugely intoxicating.

The moment you voice your intention to recognise Source is the moment you reignite. So, turn yourself on! Feel Source lift your spirits. Recall you are light.

To love Source, which is the extraordinary, profound, divine energy that exists in all things, is to see it everywhere: in cute furry animals, in the eyes of the sick, in garden blooms, in the hearts of the despairing, in the innocence of children, in the togetherness of friends, and in *everything else in between that is far less Hallmark-y.* The love of the Divine is something you can take with you wherever you go. A brilliant way to honour others is to speak to everyone as though you are conversing with God ... *because you are. God is in all things. It is all God!*

So, back to your original question, Sweet Child O' Mine. Source is utterly real — more real than the nose on your face, and more real than your three-dimensional stage show. Source is not just available to you. It is *part* of you. You know this already at a very deep level, otherwise you would never have initiated this conversation with me in the first place. For now, we shall leave it at that.

Till next time, great goddess, may the Source be with you.

Exercise: How can you experience Source?

No matter how crazy-busy, draining or overwhelming your life is, if you choose to reconnect with Source, you will dynamically plug into this energy, even in the midst of calamity. So, let's try it now. First, say:

'I choose to ignite the divine energy within me.'

Today, remind yourself as often as you can that Source is with you, in you, around you, in every molecule, right here, right now. You are animated by it. You are God in action. It *lives* you. Think about that for a moment to let it sink in.

Source—the omniscient creator of the known and unknown universe; that which possesses incomparable power and a love so great that it has the potential to blow you away—is *here* with you *now*.

This is such a fascinating, simple, yet explosive little exercise that I recommend you practise it often, particularly when your next drama hits. By remembering the big picture, life's demands will hopefully take their rightful place.

Good God, you are awesome!

Cheat Sheet: Source

- Source is real.
- Source is exhilarating, dynamic, infinite, benevolent, joyful, beautiful, ecstatic, peaceful, powerful, expansive, curious, perfect, graceful, active, loving, compassionate, omniscient, gentle, tender and wholly available to you.
- Source is the antithesis of an angry, vengeful god.
- Source doesn't love you more if you do something 'right' or withhold love if you do something 'wrong'.
- Source consistently holds you in its awareness and regards you as infinitely precious.
- Source loves, honours and respects you in the same way it loves, honours and respects itself.
- Source loves, honours and respects its own creation, like a parent loves its child.
- You are one with Source, and Source is one with you.
- You are a crucial, irreplaceable and integral element that has been carefully woven into the fabric of the universe.
- Source energy thrives in your heart.
- Source energy is present during times of despair.
- Converse with each individual as though you are conversing with God ... because you are.
- You were born to love.

Chapter 6. *Love*

Dear Blob,

Your words excite me as much as they scare me. When you mentioned me 'switching on' before, I actually felt it, so let's see if we can turn things up a notch or two.

If you know me as well as I think you do, you're probably aware that I've been posing this next burning question for most of my life: **What is love?**

Yup, **the mysterious 'L' word** that makes so little sense. **Why is love so elusive, perplexing, wonderful and painful?**

Any light you can shed on this subject would be greatly appreciated.

With kindest regards,
Ludicrous Love Luddite

Dear Love-Filled Life-Form,

Greetings to you on this illustrious day.

Of course I knew you were bursting to ask me this one! I'm only surprised that it took you this long. It is another big one, so allow me a moment to draw an unnecessary breath before we plunge in.

Okay. Here we go.

Love: Everything possesses energy, including your favourite thing, love. Like Source, love is a glorious force that pulses at the heart of all things. It permeates the known universe and beyond. It is the glue that binds. It connects us all. It swathes the multiverse in softness. It is the fire in the furnace of the cosmos. It is the active element of Source. It is its divine spark.

If Source were the ocean, then love would be its currents. If Source were the sun, then love would be its rays. If it were the moon, then love would be its luminosity. Even the dance between the sun and moon is an expression of love, which returns us to connection.

Source and love are one and the same. Love is God in motion, and even though there are no words potent enough to relay the perfection of love, it is an energy that inspires kindness, openness, gentleness, care, compassion, vitality, freedom and patience. It is devoid of fear and is ever-present whether or not the ego is aware, regardless of what's going on, regardless of what chaos abounds and regardless of whether you choose to be attuned to it or not.

The space that you occupy right now is teeming with love. You are continuously surrounded by it, driven by it, embodying it and moving through it. You, my dear, are the stuff of love, and one of the greatest things you will ever realise is that you *are* love. You are an expression of universal love. I have one word for you, and that's ... *wow*! Doesn't that just blow you away?

It does! But as a humble human, I also find it baffling.

What can I do with this love of which you speak?

My goodness! So much that I don't know where to start!

Because you are made of love, you are in a fabulous position to extend it to others in many different ways: through listening to somebody in pain, respecting your fellows, allowing others to be who they are, reserving your judgement, offering compassion, being kind and considerate, making dinner for a friend, smiling at strangers, offering your seat, picking up rubbish, allowing a driver into your lane (rather than extending a finger) ... and on and on it goes.

I ask you to cast your mind back to the last loving act you performed and watch yourself in action through your mind's eye. First of all, I liked what you were wearing that day, although I was slightly

....

unconvinced by the scarf. Secondly, as you observe yourself offering love on that occasion, imagine shimmering waves of colour radiating from your being. Hear a delicious melody humming from you that can almost be tasted. See energy flowing *from* you and *through* you, heightening the vibration of everything around you.

From up here, that's what we see whenever you act lovingly. We see tendrils of vast, beautiful energy undulating, pulsating and affecting everything around you as it emanates into the cosmos. *That's* love. That's you acting as a conduit to love. And I can't stress enough how *real* it is and how often we see it. There are literally millions upon millions of loving acts being performed right now as we speak. It's just that your world seems fixated by the opposite, so much so that I'm beginning to wonder if Earth needs a new PR manager!

But to be clear, we blobs know love as a gorgeous, organic 'thing' that thrives in the universe, which you have every opportunity to exude, receive, explore and use to positive effect.

Should you accept this, you will open yourself up to heightened awareness, bliss, euphoria, joy, elation, jubilation, rapture, ecstasy, exaltation, contentment, serenity, satisfaction, acceptance, expansion, peace, joy, harmony, tranquillity, safety, well-being, happiness, compassion, kindness, benevolence, fulfilment and inspiration. And tell me you don't want a little piece of *that* action!

I do! I guess it's easy to forget just how beautiful love is, so thank you for reminding me. I only wish I was a more loving person. **Try as I might, it's hard to love down here sometimes, you know?**

I know, Dear One. I know only too well. But even if you don't always feel loving, you are *inherently* loving, okay? You *are* love. It is the essence of you. Strip away the other attributes that you identify with—such as being a quirky, orange juice-slurping author riddled with earwax and wayward emotions who 'tries' to love—and you are left with a pure, loving being. *That is you!* Can you feel the truth of what I'm saying? Can you feel the truth of who you really are? Try sitting with it for a moment to enjoy the deliciousness. The more you do, the easier it will be to love not only yourself, but everything, full stop, amen, because you will come to see that it is as intrinsic to you as it is to everyone else. It is abundantly available for all to share.

By 'intrinsic' I mean that love isn't something you need to strain over to create. It already exists. There is no need to radically change anything to experience it. It is more about nuzzling up to who you already are, transcending and sending a silent shout-out to Source along the lines of, 'Help me to demonstrate more of this scrumptiousness in any way I can. *Help me to see that I am love!*'

I'm telling you, love moves through you. It is your job to tune into it ... and why wouldn't you want to? Why wouldn't you choose to feel it wash through you and bask in its radiance?

We blobs sometimes find it difficult to comprehend that giving and receiving love on your planet is so hard, but, hey, we're not there. We're sitting up here with our popcorn musing over how confusing it must be to be constantly surrounded by madness. However, we do know that it would be hugely beneficial if you continually reminded yourselves that *you are fundamentally loving.* You were created that way. It is natural for you to love. It is unnatural for you *not* to.

I'm sorry, Blob, but it's hard to buy into that when you are always **poised for unloving acts being perpetrated against you**. We can't help but be drawn and ready for attack a lot of the time. **That's natural, surely?**

It is natural for your animal self to feel the need to defend itself, yes. But let me remind you that you are a spirit in the material world. You are completely safe. You are enduringly loved. In fact, you are loved by Source whether you are poised for attack or not, and whether your fears are 'real' or imagined. Let me also remind you that you are immortal and will be loved forever, regardless of what is playing out in your dreamlike reality.

If you are able to still yourself for a while, you will experience the profound vastness in which you exist and see just how safe you really are. The vastness is comprised of love. In it you belong. From the grandest perspective there is, you exist in a place of safety. How wonderful is *that*? How wonderful is love?

Therefore, all you need is love. All is full of love. Love is all around. Heck, I could fill the rest of this book with song titles and verses and it still wouldn't be enough to capture the magnitude of what can barely be described with words. Nevertheless, I must reiterate: regardless of your fears and actions, or those of others, love is everywhere. It exists in, above and beyond all situations. Whatever pops into your head to counter this is the very thing that prohibits you from seeing the truth for what it is. It prohibits you from surpassing the illusions of fear and hate.

I watch your ego waste a great deal of time being afraid and finding fault with your face, hair, arms, stomach, clothes, food, home, relationships, job, devices, sentence structure, society and on and on it goes. You never stop appraising yourself, others, life and the world in unloving ways. It is your ego that erects these barriers and distracts you from the love that abounds.

If it is your hope to gain your ego's approval and everyone else's through buying into lower vibrational fiction, you will never feel love to the degree you deserve, which is love of the highest order. And if you fail to pull your awareness from where it is currently fixed, you will never experience love to the extent that you can.

Connecting with universal love will supply you with the satisfaction that often seems just out of reach. Nothing else will grant you this sense of completion. Not a new iPad. Not a new lover. Not a new kitten. Just lovely love, which you already possess in spades and which flickers within you like an eternal flame. It makes sense, then, that you do all in your power to tap into your essence and experience it in all its glory.

Keep doing what you're doing now. Keep drawing your awareness to the fact that *you are love*. Keep reminding yourself. Keep nurturing the seedling in your heart that is poised to bloom into an explosion of joy. Keep reminding yourself that of everything that transpires in your lifetime, love is all that matters. Not how well you did at school. Not how brilliantly you excelled in your career. Not how straight your teeth became after an orthodontic intervention. Not how much money you accrued or how well your curtains matched the carpet! The only thing that you will take to the grave is the merit of your actions—how well you served yourself and others—which boils down to one thing, which is, you guessed it, *love*!

I hear what you're saying, Blob, and now I feel awful for all the times I've acted like an unloving, self-serving cow. **What happens when I slip up and I'm not very nice?**

Darling, when you act unlovingly, you act out of fear. On those occasions, your energy becomes blocked and your life feels draining, yet your non-loving actions seem acceptable to you because, well, you can't help but notice that the world abounds with 'morons' (as I've heard you phrase it). When you find yourself arriving at this conclusion, it may be helpful to remember that you are judging others' egos via your own ego rather than noticing others' inherent godliness, which they may be blind to themselves.

Granted, you can't exactly be blamed for your misconceptions when so many people are ego projecting all over the place. Folks' obliviousness to their own sweet divinity is rife where you are. But in truth, behind every façade is an energetic being that wants to give and receive love just as much as the next person; a being that is a sliver of Source having an earthly experience, whether they know it or not, as we touched on before.

However, on those occasions when you catch yourself being unloving, rather than lamenting that you're not being as open-hearted as you can, say to yourself, 'I am open to love and doing my best to recognise it in the person before me.' Remember, love is a glorious force that pulsates in and out of everything. By permitting it to enter all situations, you are allowing it to move things along harmoniously rather than permitting your ego to barge in and manipulate matters pursuant to its whims.

The ultimate objective, of course, is to love everyone and everything unconditionally, not just the select few whom you deem worthy. To love unconditionally is to love everyone who crosses your path. I can see you now going cross-eyed and finding it hard to believe that this is even possible, but it is. It *is* possible for true love to generate from you and be extended to whomever is before you.

Yes, love has the capacity to accomplish the seemingly impossible. It can strongly influence how you view the world, your fellow inhabitants, and how they view themselves, too.

So we're talking about **unconditional love** now. I hear that term so often that it kind of aggravates me. **What does it mean?**

My sweet, unconditional love is that which is given without reservation or expectation. It is free of entrapment and restriction. It is devoid of fear and control. It comes with no hidden agendas. The giver of unconditional love delights in the giving and expects nothing in return. In fact, the giver wants to give *more* because the act of giving is so titillating and delicious! This is the type of love we blobs see arcing from your planet and extending into the far reaches of the cosmos.

On the flipside, conditional love is giving in the hope of receiving. It makes you and/or the recipient of your 'affections' vulnerable and diminishes the power of all concerned. If you give in the hope that others will return the favour and they *do*, then that's all well and good. But if they don't, you are bound to feel angry, cheated, put out and used. In both scenarios, your fulfilment depends on how others react to your offerings, and sadly, it doesn't get much more conditional than that!

But, for giggles, let's say that divine love is eternally present and everywhere, as I keep insisting. Let's say there is a reservoir of love that will never run dry and never be withheld from anyone or anything. If that's true, and I assure you it is, it stands to reason that you can experience unconditional love in every moment without need for anyone to do your bidding or assure you that you are great, valued, awesome or anything else that 'proves' that you matter.

Unconditional love is given generously and consistently. I don't mean to cast aspersions here, but you have only managed to dole out

....

love in limited dispatches for the most part because (a) you can't give what you don't have—and by that I refer to self-love—and (b) you have never felt secure enough to give love unconditionally for fear of being hurt. This will continue until you surrender your ego to the truth of who you are. However, there will come a day when you will arrive at the understanding that security exists in its most absolute form smack bang at the centre of you.

How do I get to that amazing place, then?

Actually, my phrasing around you 'arriving' wasn't ideal because, in reality, you are already 'there'. I only speak in terms of you reaching a destination to accommodate your linear way of thinking. It may sound cryptic, and I don't mean to go all Yoda on you, but as I intimated earlier, Source love is at the centre of you. Again, you are already connected to love. You are already love. You are already divine. So you don't have to 'get' anywhere other than to a place of acceptance.

If you delve into this concept enough, you will notice your fears being gently replaced by something so gentle and phenomenal that it defies description. I therefore suggest that you extract yourself from the ever-changing, unreliable outer world and plug yourself into your consistent, ever-reliable inner world. That is where you will experience love and safety to a degree that you have not known before, where true peace reigns and your heart knows calm.

Exploring your inner world is best carried out gracefully. Being a generously loving individual does not come about through self-flagellation! Remember, love is your natural state and is well worth the discovery. Once you recall who you are, you will more easily build upon that foundation.

So, in closing, focusing on love is yet another choice for you to

....

make. If you decide to nurture your kind and beautiful nature, then experiencing it, sharing it and playing with it will become your greatest joy. You will see for yourself that love is generous, unconditional, boundless, powerful, wondrous and abundantly available to you. It is what you are. I could talk about this for the rest of your life, but it is time to move on as I sense another of your axis-shifting questions indicating a topic change, which excites me no end.

As I pause now full of loving anticipation, I urge you to ask yourself in the interim: 'In how many ways can I love today?'

Exercise: How can you love?

Loving yourself is the crucial first step in loving unconditionally, and this little exercise is one of the simplest things you can do.

By repeating 'I love myself', you flex your self-love muscle, which brings you that little bit closer to experiencing your true self and resonating with love in ways most profound. So, say to yourself now:

'I love myself.'

Taste the words in your mouth. How do they make you feel? Uncomfortable or silly? Do you feel as though you're lying to yourself or being insincere? Or do you notice something stirring within you that feels really good — something true, pure, natural and wonderful?

We are aiming for the latter, of course, as that's the genuine deal.

Take heed of your reactions and try to keep self-love at the forefront of your mind today (or, rather, always). Keep returning to the idea till you feel it vibrating at the nucleus of your cells and warming your being as you stride through the world.

Don't forget: *you are love.*

Cheat Sheet: Love

- Love is a vast, beautiful energy that impacts everything in the universe.
- Love is the fire in the furnace of the cosmos.
- Love is God in motion.
- Love is an energy that connects all things.
- Love pulses in and around everything.
- Love is ever-present.
- Love inspires softness, compassion, kindness, generosity, vitality, openness, patience and freedom.
- Love opens up the possibility of heightened states of awareness, bliss, euphoria, joy, elation, jubilation, rapture, ecstasy, exaltation, contentment, serenity, satisfaction, acceptance, expansion, peace, joy, harmony, tranquillity, safety, well-being, happiness, compassion, kindness, benevolence, fulfilment and inspiration.
- Love is devoid of fear.
- Love is all that matters.
- You are a being of love.
- The love inside you has the capacity to quench all that you crave.
- It is natural for you to love; it is unnatural for you not to.
- Your natural energy flow is curbed when you act unlovingly.
- Behind every ego is an energetic being that wants to give and receive love.
- Unconditional love means loving all who cross your path.
- Genuine love means giving without expectation.
- Giving love in the hope of receiving is conditional.
- Divine love is ever-present to remind you that you are valued and treasured beyond your wildest dreams.

....

- In how many ways can you love today?
- You were born to love.

Chapter 7. **Romance**

Dearest Blob,

I'm sorry for interrupting you again. I need to stop doing that!

But given that I have, I repeat that I do not particularly feel like an unlimited loving being. I just don't. I feel closer to a snarly, embittered old cat lady. I'm sad about that and I will do my best to do what you suggest in relation to remembering my (alleged) loving nature.

Meanwhile, I couldn't help but notice that you side-stepped one of my all-time favourite subjects: romance. When I asked about love, that was what I was talking about. So ...

What about romantic love?

And why did you skip it?

Love,

Not-So-New-Romantic

Dear Not-So-New-Romantic ... who still secretly indulges in eighties new wave band Duran Duran. (Yes, *we know!*)

Don't think I didn't realise that romantic love was at the forefront of your mind when you posed your last question, given that you used the words *elusive, perplexing, wonderful* and *painful*. However, the only adjective in that sequence that applies to genuine love is *wonderful*, and I hope you still love me by the end of this conversation, because it may be less 'romantic' than you hope!

The topic of love can be broken down into two parts. First, there is love, as in the most explosive force in the universe that I have just finished describing. Then there is romantic love, as in that which quickens the heart and provides inspiration for modern-day crooners.

....

So, as per your request, let us speak of that now.

Romantic relationships usually begin with a splash of euphoria. *Yippee!* You've finally found somebody who *gets* you, who will give you the time of day, who will love you forever and gaze into your eyes as you both ingest food. This special someone is dining with you for more than the express purpose of feeding themselves to stay alive. They actually *dig* you!

As this is playing out, the intoxicating feelings you are experiencing are twofold. One, you are enjoying attraction, which is the Universe's invitation to solve another piece of the puzzle by placing you in circumstances that will help you to heal, serve and grow through relating with another. Two, you are experiencing warm and fuzzy feelings that are an expression of Love with a capital *L* awakening inside you.

What you don't realise when you are falling in love is that it is *you* who flicks on your heart's switch and not the object of your desire. It is also *you* who recognises the divine nature of the person with whom you are falling in love with. While others might perceive your new lover to be ordinary, fallible and flatulent, romantic love enables you to see past that. Through your doting gaze, you see an angel—nay, a god—which is much closer to the truth of who you *both* are. But, again, it is *you* who recognises this. The loving feelings being generated are coming from the mystical and vast expansiveness of *you*.

When you participate in the dance of romance in a more enlightened way, you are remembering your spiritual nature and that of your partner. Committing to a loving relationship is really you saying, 'I've seen the truth of who you are slip past our respective egos and I like what I saw. I would like to see more, thanks. You are truly divine!' That's love. That is *true* love: recognising the divinity in your loved one.

· · · · · · · · · · · · ·

When you realise there is no separation between you and your lover, you see your finest self being reflected back at you. This is how it usually feels when you first fall in love, and you know this feeling well. In the infancy of your relationships, you have felt the bliss of non-separation. You have sensed that you have finally found someone with whom you can share your life—the ups, downs, wins, losses and dreams—and your loved one is there to meet you halfway and share themselves, too.

With the veil of separation lifted, you find yourself calmer, more flexible, more accepting and tolerant, and for as long as you carry these feelings, situations that would ordinarily drive you nuts fade into the background. The world seems more palatable. You start skipping through daisies. Life becomes truly enchanting!

I assure you that these feelings are valid. They are not delusional trickery. They do not simply represent sexual anticipation before the bubble bursts. When you are falling in love in a healthy way, you are experiencing the bliss of joining with another and recognising the wonder, divinity and worth of your lover and yourself.

Romantic love is, therefore, a golden opportunity to experience your true self and that of your partner. It is an absolute gift.

But why is it so hard to sustain the amazing feelings that you've just described?

Ah, yes. *That.* Let me explain.

As the euphoria of your new love subsides, you may begin to sense a teeny drop of reservation creeping in. You begin to question. You begin to judge. You see little flaws in your partner that you didn't notice before, ones that you're not sure you'll be able to tolerate for the rest of your life. You start second-guessing. You judge a little more, which builds over time. You then start searching for evidence that your partner deserves your love or still loves you. You begin withholding your love. You set little tests, and chances are your partner is doing the same thing too. So, what's going on?

It is the return of the Great Separation! A shadow has been cast!

So, let us go back to the beginning.

When you and the apple of your eye first meet, you start merging at a deep, soul level. Your yearning for divine union is being satisfied, and so mighty is the momentum, that the voice of judgement is silenced. However, as time marches on, its whininess can be heard, quietly at first, but growing in volume. The inner judge begins criticising the fact that your partner isn't quite doing things as he or she ought to; they're falling just shy of the mark; their beliefs aren't quite as right as yours are; their toes aren't quite to your liking. In other words, *your ego has commandeered the steering wheel*!

And here is the clincher: when you hope that your partner will change, *that isn't love*. Attempting to coerce them into doing your bidding *isn't love either*. These are distorted manipulations of love, and the ego enjoys nothing more than cultivating such things. It thrives on criticism, revenge, anger, regret, annoyance and all things fear-based. Its definition of 'love' orbits around control, superiority, inferiority, ownership, clinginess, selfishness and jealousy. It can never wholly give.

The ego devotes significant time to ruminating over how much better off you would be if only your significant other had the common decency to behave in a certain way; how it might even be better if they vanished altogether. But rather than externalising and relying on your beloved to change, *it would be far wiser to nurture the love within,* thus lifting your vibration and, hopefully, that of your partner, too.

So, how do I keep my romances alive, then?

By nurturing the love within!

You can also carefully examine how you are relating to your partner. Be accountable. Rather than expecting them to change, focus on their positive attributes and heal and grow *yourself*. Nurture the tenderness within. Exercise unconditional love. Be alert for the judge. Be wary of the condemning voice that belongs to the part of you that strolls up and down the corridors of your mind with a clipboard in hand, evaluating your lover's every move. Return to how you felt at the beginning of your relationship, when you gazed into your dreamboat's eyes ... *and saw God*!

Remember, unconditional love is when you see another's divinity and don't wish for them to change; when you see another's 'whole-liness' and don't seek to possess them; when you simply choose to *be* with someone for the sake of *being*. Unconditional love is transparent, open and accepting of others for who they are without subclauses and disclaimers. It is never curbed or withheld.

It's a lovely idea, Blob, and I don't mean to be a downer, but why bother? **Why are we so desperate to be in** romantic **relationships** in the first place when history shows that they **are rife with pitfalls and danger?**

Ah. The answer to that is an extension of what I've already said, though it's slightly more weird-sounding, so I'm pleased that you asked!

Every relationship is a learning opportunity. How you choose to relate to another helps to evolve you into whomever you want to be.

....

Your quest to explore love through one-on-one relationships is also a metaphor for your yearning to reconnect with the Divine. There is a part of you that thinks you forfeited this connection when you were born into this life. Romantic love, devoid of ego, therefore provides you with a taste of the connection you yearn for.

All the judgement you have about yourself, your partner, your life and everyone in it undermines your efforts to re-experience oneness. Your ego lures you in and out of relationships, hinting that the *next* one might be 'it', that if you dump your current beau, you might just stumble across 'the One'. Only the ego's concept of what that constitutes is generally a non-attainable ideal.

Unless you are in a highly destructive relationship—and I speak here of physical and psychological violence—it isn't necessary to move from one person to the next in the hope of finding 'the One'. Bouncing from relationship to relationship can distract you from realising the love that you are, and if you are not exercising self-love, chances are the cycle will continue till your bones hit the grave. You will succeed only in having entertained the same character in a slightly different guise each time. And you deserve so much more than that. You deserve to burst through every barrier that circumvents your experience of love so that you can more easily share it.

You succeed in this by understanding *yourself* as the source of your experience. You take responsibility. You step up. You be open-hearted, passionate and fearless. You remind yourself that you incarnated to love and be loved. You remind yourself that you are worthy. You shine the love you have within you unreservedly.

You forgive. You see past other people's weaknesses, but you never dim yourself down. You never water down your power, grace, perfection, loveliness or wisdom. You *never* tolerate deception, abuse or bear the brunt of another's pain if it defiles you. All relationships arc lessons. The lesson can be to move on.

....

However, I remind you that love perennially courses through you, whether you turn your awareness to it or not, and *this* is the love that you crave, not that which is sought through inauthentic relationships or Tinder dalliances where you choose the value of a prospective date by the breadth of their chest! We find it sad that more and more people are closing their hearts because they regard respectfully relating to others as too much hard work rather than an opportunity to explore the purest energy form that there is.

If I may put forward my two blob's worth, if humans put as much effort into exploring each other's souls as they do each other's bodies, the world would be a lot less egocentric. When it comes to seeking genuine love, the focus should be on the spirit of the person before you, not on how well stacked their atoms are to create their outer shell!

I realise that this goes against the grain of just about everything you have been taught. Think of all the love songs, movies and romance novels that support the idea that you can only ever be fulfilled by the love of a Venus or Adonis. To think otherwise even sounds a tad boring. After all, where's the fun in *not* falling into the arms of a robust farmhand? But the point I am trying to make is *the more you connect with the love inside you, the more others can, too.*

True mastery lies in feeling safe, secure, understood, serene and loved *internally*, to bathe blissfully in your own wonder and worth, and to share that with others. You are only in a position to truly love somebody while you are in this state anyway because you are not asking anyone to fulfil you in a way that only you can.

Ask someone else to do the loving for you and—I'm sorry to say—they will likely let you down. Only *you* can wholly love yourself, and this places you in a wonderful position of power. When you give yourself what you've pleaded the world to give you, the jig is up. One of life's greatest ironies is that when you genuinely love yourself, you will more easily receive love.

I am not suggesting that if you wholly love yourself, you will never have need of another. I am also not suggesting that only one important relationship will matter in your life. *All* relationships are important, whether they are short and sweet or long and enduring. While size doesn't matter, *relationships do*—every single one of them—for every interaction you have with another person is an opportunity to love and grow.

When it comes to long-term relationships, if self-love and wisdom well from your depths and those of your partner, then *fabulous*! The explosion of two people sharing this understanding can be as mind-blowing as it can be heart-melting. On those occasions where two worlds collide—or, rather, merge—we blobs throw our wildest parties. When two people *get* what I'm talking about and *live* it, the energy exchanged is sufficient to quake the heavens, and, as electro-pop wizards Depeche Mode once said, I just can't get enough!

Despite the breakup statistics, it *is* possible to remain in a sustained relationship with a beautiful partner and experience higher love. It *is* possible to revel in peace and harmony, entertain shared dreams and jointly create. By extending unconditional love rather than trepidation, you can attract someone with whom you can share a haven of safety, trust, respect and mutual admiration. You can grow together.

So, when you are in a relationship, ask yourself if it is honouring all of the above. Is it honouring you and your precious soul? Is it honouring the one with whom you are sharing your life? How much innocence are you willing to see in your partner's eyes? How much of your sweetness are you willing to reveal? How much are you withholding and willing to examine? How much can you appreciate your betrothed for the insights they provide? How much fear and doubt are you willing to suspend? How far are you willing to travel to treat your beloved as you wish to be treated yourself? How far are you willing to go to explore the sublime depths of love?

In many ways, you are courting aspects of yourself when you are with another person, which is all the more reason to love yourself and your partner as hard as you can. If you keep this in mind, it becomes more about loving yourself while your partner shows you what you most need to see. Opportunities will present themselves that allow you to self-improve. It becomes about seeing your lover and yourself as divine beings and treating yourselves accordingly — with love and respect.

I guess that's food for thought, but it begs the question, given my shoddy relationships to date. **Have I not loved myself enough to allow others to love me back?**

Dear One, for the most part, you have believed that you will only experience love if another bestows it upon you. You have gone through your fair share of romances and yet have only had transitory experiences of what we would call love.

You have had your heart broken. You have had your body broken. You have withheld love and entered doomed relationships. In your mind, this has confirmed that you cannot rely on anybody. It has caused you to close off your heart. Yet you have not only survived, but evolved enough to see love more clearly when it has genuinely presented itself. It has shown you that love and security first come from within. You have, therefore, proven my point!

So, let us wind things up. Unfortunately, your world has been teaching you an inaccurate method of attaining what you already have. The global fixation on romantic love steeped in external acquisition, fear and egotism threatens to further cripple your planet.

....

The judgement of your partner can eclipse your heart, as can thoughts of being unlovable and not good enough. If you can swap these fallacies for the truth of who you really are, a new dynamic will dawn.

The extent to which you drop the care of your fragile emotions into the hands of another in the hope that they will keep you safe is the extent to which you are setting yourself up for failure.

Genuine love doesn't fade in and out or switch on and off. It prevails. You maintain a loving state by staying alert for love in your world and prioritising it as the lens through which you see.

If you are on the lookout for signs of love and light in your life, you will notice them more. And they are *there.* They are always there, even though you may need to squint your eyes sometimes to see them!

You absolutely, unequivocally deserve to experience love in its every conceivable form — unconditionally, exquisitely, purely and magically.

Your soul uses everything, including relationships, to love, grow and expand. It does whatever it can to flourish, so be open, courageous and generous with your love, knowing that *I* love you truly, madly, deeply, and always will.

Exercise: How can you feel the love?

How can you experience true love? *By feeling it right now, in this moment.*

Begin by becoming quiet. As you breathe deeply, drop down into your heart centre and become gently aware of the everlasting love that exists there. Stay with your breath. Expand your lungs. Expand your chest. Lengthen your spine. Fill your lungs with each new breath. Imagine your whole body expanding. Sense your heart shining like a beacon through any uncertainty.

Now, keep your awareness there. If you catch yourself thinking unproductive thoughts, return your awareness to your heart. Allow yourself to linger there for a while, then whisper to yourself:

'I pay attention to my heart while my heart focuses on Love.'

Stay with anything that arises. Feel your heart warming. Then slowly, slowly begin generating love. Feel love and compassion for yourself. Gently offer that feeling to people you know, people you don't know and ultimately *everyone.*

Take your time, relish the ritual and enjoy the sensations. If you're guided by love, then you cannot go wrong.

The more you generate love, the more you will draw it to yourself, be it romantic love or love in any form.

Cheat Sheet: Romance

- Attraction is the Universe's invitation to accept another piece of the puzzle to help you heal and grow.
- Your soul uses everything, including romantic partnerships, to experience love.
- Romantic love can help you to feel connected to All That Is.
- Love yourself rather than expecting somebody else to do it for you.
- The extent to which you give the care of your fragile emotions to another is the extent to which you set yourself up for failure.
- When you fall in love, the focus should be on the spirit before you rather than a person's anatomical structure!
- When you fall in love, it is you who flicks on the switch.
- When you fall in love, gaze into your lover's eyes ... and see God.
- Falling in love offers the opportunity to recognise another's divinity.
- Falling in love is remembering your spiritual truth and that of your partner.
- Ego 'love' involves control, ownership, clinginess, selfishness and jealousy.
- Unconditional love is transparent, open and accepting.
- Be open-hearted, passionate and fearless.
- Be alert for the judge.
- Take responsibility.
- Step up.
- Know that you are worthy.
- The love that you seek is within *and* without.
- You were born to love.

Chapter 8.

Separation and Illusion

Dear Blob,

Thanks a million for indulging me on the romance front. My robust farmhand and I found it incredibly insightful as we plucked strands of hay from each other's hair!

However, you have peppered much of our conversation with the words 'separation' and 'illusion', so I'm now wondering if you wouldn't mind elaborating on this a little more. **What do you mean by *separation and illusion*?**

Merci beaucoup for being so fab.

Yours, Universal Star Child ... (or something)

Dear Universal Super Star,

Ah, defining separation and illusion. Such a simple request, so please, sit back and relax as I describe mind-bending concepts and the nature of reality in forty or so easy-to-read paragraphs!

First off, let me tackle illusion. You are immortal. You are timeless. You are love. You are an element of Source. Any concept outside of this is pretty much illusory, and mostly of your own making, particularly anything that suggests you are less than empowered or have no hope of breaking free.

Pardon the quick interruption. **It's all well and good to say that everything outside of that is a big, fat illusion, but my life certainly** feels real. I'm still a person flapping about, paying bills, shopping, cooking and cleaning, and those bins aren't going to empty themselves!

You are right. And one of the most sage pieces of advice that I will ever dispense to you is ... *don't forget bin night on Monday*!

In all seriousness, though, the concept of illusion is difficult to integrate into your current paradigm, so let's try again.

Everything in your world seems solid and real. You see things, hear things, taste things and touch things. But from where I float, your 'reality' is closer to a movie in which you star and the people around you either co-star or play minor roles. At times, your film fits the drama genre, though more often than not, it is closer to a comedy, which I mean with no disrespect!

In the grand scheme of things, your life and what you do with it matter immensely, and you are living your existence for a very valid reason, which we will get into more later. For now, let's just say that your 'movie' contains strong adult themes and coarse language, but remains highly purposeful and interactive as you grow with your fellow cast-members.

However, the only things of lasting significance in your movie are story lines involving how well you treated others, how much you loved, how much you served, how much you evolved and how far you travelled in terms of enlightenment. That is why you took human form and immersed yourself in this performance in the first place: to love, serve and grow. These are the only things that you will reflect upon when your number is up. They are what you will be remembered for. They are all that matter.

Everything else is fundamentally illusory, like fast-fading fragments of a once-vivid dream. I know that this scares you, or at least causes your brain to wobble, but it's true. One day your life will be over, and you will vanish as though you never existed. Of course, being immortal, that's not the case, but there is a slight chance that you won't be a household name in a thousand years' time.

I said *slight.* [*Cough.*]

Anyway, that's what I mean by illusion. In your realm, huge emphasis is placed on things of little significance—money, beauty, power, one-upmanship, usurpation, fame, possessions, ladder-climbing—when the only thing that matters is love.

Now, stay with me as we move onto the subject of separation.

Separation is the illusion that you are unplugged from your fellow beings and the universe. While it may be true that you seem to be having an individual experience while trapped in a bag of bones, honouring bin night, that is the tiniest piece of an infinite puzzle. There is inordinately more texture to who you are and what your life is about.

As I keep saying, you are *of* Source. You are never separate from it, even though you're slinking about thinking you're a unique, sassy mammal praying for the comeback of jacket-tassels. You are definitely unique — nobody can argue with that. But you are not separate from that from which you came. Nor are you separate from your fellow human beings or anything else in the multiverse, for *everything* originates from Source and is therefore connected. It's another big concept, but it means that 'you' and 'I' are one, which technically means that I'm talking to myself!

Or I'm talking to myself! **But how can it be that we are one and connected when I feel so individual?**

Ah! If only I had a chin to tap while figuring out the best way to analogise this.

....

Okay, I've got it.

Picture a large body of water, like an ocean. See yourself standing at the shore, reaching down and scooping out a cup of water. From that cup, imagine procuring a droplet. Now, obviously, each measure of liquid along that chain remains part of the sea. Each drop has originated from the same source and always will. Each tiny droplet is connected by virtue of its origins.

Do you see where I'm going here? In this analogy, the ocean is Source, and you and all beings are the droplets. You are all part of the same Source. You are all part of the same fabric. You are all cut from the same cloth. And now that we've moved onto textiles, allow me to stretch the metaphor in another direction.

Imagine divine energy as being powerfully present, light-filled and everywhere. Now, picture yourself donning a shroud that cuts you off from this truth. The shroud creates an illusion of there being two separate things: you 'in here' and everything 'out there'. Now, imagine your shroud flapping about, hell-bent on capturing your attention.

'Hey, check me out! I'm a shroud! *I'm a shroud!* Watch me flap about in the breeze! *Yippee!'*

Meanwhile, the all-but-forgotten energy 'outside' is still there, patiently undulating, while your irritating shroud continues to entrance you into forgetting that there is a bigger picture beyond it.

Despite the phenomenal power around you, you are mesmerised by the shroud, either admiring it or critiquing it. All the magnificence of the universe is right there in front of you, but there you are, massaging your forehead and muttering, 'Oh my God. The shroud just moved. Did you see that? And look at that crease. It needs a good iron.'

You focus on, and obsess over, the shroud. You attempt to adjust it in the hope that it will someday become the greatest shroud of all time. *You keep attempting to make sense of the shroud when the shroud makes no sense at all!*

If you hadn't already guessed, the shroud symbolises your sense of separation as imposed by the ego. It tricks you into believing that you, the Divine and everyone else are in no way connected.

I would therefore like to say: *Forget the flapping shroud, for flap's sake! It distracts you no end and can never be made perfect within your illusion!*

Instead, try concentrating on the fact that phenomenal divine energy abounds, of which you and everything else is a part.

Stop dwelling on a shroud that has you believing that trivialities matter, that you are separate from Source and your fellow people. Catch yourself out and, well, just stop it! I've tried to goad you into doing this a little at a time because I know how easily distracted you can be. But *please* quit the shroud obsession. *Please!* It is for your own good and the good of All Things.

Focus instead on your inherent power. I know it sounds spacey, but, OMG, you are literally bursting with divine energy and you don't even know it! Your 'inner' God is as powerful as your 'outer'. They are one and the same. You are a *powerhouse.* So think not of the shroud as it makes a grab for your attention. Rather, think about that which really matters: that you are a heavenly, serene, living and breathing wonder capable of extending vast amounts of energy in the form of inexorable love. You are more than a shroud connoisseur!

Begin to choose differently. Recognise that you are connected to everyone. Know that whether you are a world leader, politician, CEO, division manager, team leader, employee, retailer, customer, mother, teacher, street sweeper or Uber driver, the way you treat others matters greatly. Every action has repercussions. The way you behave toward people creates a ripple effect. Recognise that every thought, word and deed affects the whole. And recognise that improvements to the collective *start with you.*

....

Okay, okay! I hear you. You are saying that I'm not separate from Source, or anybody or anything. But it's still a bit of a stretch for me, to recycle your fabric pun.
I still feel separate from everybody.
I'm still in a body doing my thing. I might need a little help here to get me over the line.

No worries. Let me come at it from a different direction.

You have come into this life to understand a few things, including the fact that you are divine and irrevocably connected to everyone. You are divinity gliding through ever-changing circumstances that are about as real as a dream. The only sustainable reality within your dream is *love*.

If you could wave a magic wand and remove illusion from the picture, only Source and love would remain. They are the only enduring things. And given that you and your contemporaries are of Source, you are equally enduring. You are beyond important and will never cease to be. This applies to everybody. You are all components of the one ocean.

To refresh your memory, Source is present in everything. It is in 'you' now as much as it is in 'them', and you are all joined. It is present in every circumstance and glistening in every eye. It is up to you to choose to either search for Source in every being and situation, or tune into separation, which is the false idea that you are alone, different, vulnerable and cut off from the next gal or guy.

Yes, you are seemingly doing your own thing in that funky body of yours, but it would help to draw your awareness away from the insular illusion and focus on the grand reality that encompasses the intricate interconnectedness of all beings. While you may seem to be 'flying solo', you remain an integral piece of an expansive puzzle, completing the most exquisite creation ever!

I'm no fool, by the way. I know what you're thinking. You're thinking that connecting with God and all those 'losers' out there is a far cry from sexy. It's not something you'd care to add to your LinkedIn profile or share with a gym buddy anytime soon. You fear that letting go of your staunch belief in singularity will deem you a freak. It also throws up the concern that if you really are all connected, then you might actually have to start loving everyone — *brrghhhh!*

But I guarantee that living a life disconnected from oneness, cut off from Source and those around you, isn't worth the pain that it causes — and it is *this* that causes all the pain in the world. The whole point of me floating about in your head is to remind you of this. Thankfully, I know that you will reach a stage where you will do whatever it takes to re-experience oneness and set yourself free. In fact, I see it happening as we speak.

To help you on your way, I want to remind you that this second is jam-packed with an explosive energy that is no less present now than it will be in a year or before you draw your last breath. You and everyone else are connected *now*!

If you explore this fascinating truth with curiosity, excitement, adventure, openness, delight and love in your heart, you will begin to sense just how sublime reality really is. And by that, I mean *'real'* reality. For realsies!

But how do I experience what you're talking about short of ingesting peyote?

Holy God on a bicycle, you do make me laugh!

Well, it never hurts to meditate, which we will be discussing in greater depth further on. And it never hurts to ask for assistance, for there are mega-powerful energies—that are part of you—poised to help at every turn. Call upon 'us' to assist you in reaching new perceptive heights. Shout out that you would like to experience the interconnectedness of all things as Source supercharges each moment. Ask to feel at one with everything and to maintain that connection at all times.

Whenever you make requests like these with heartfelt sincerity, forces really do rally. I know because I am one of them. I perpetually don a sweatband in preparation for such happenings. The second you cry out for union is the moment that you light up like a Christmas tree, sending out a tractor beam that has the whole universe bending to meet you.

So, keep on striving to live from the inside out. Keep pressing for knowledge to help you break free of the story of separation. Ask delicious divinity to help open your heart, mind and eyes, and to sense what is real. Be attuned to the big You. Refocus. Remember the big picture all day, every day, knowing that the stronger the yearning, the closer it is.

I know that you long to be free. And your freedom lies in breaking free of illusion. The shedding of the stubborn shroud will only occur if you *try* — a wild proposition, I know! But every time you try to inch closer to remembering who you really are, who they really are and what this life trip is really all about—by delving within, meditating, reading, invoking, searching, investigating and loving— the closer you will be to dropping that shroud of yours once and for all. Trust me, it really doesn't suit you.

Not when you are an entity of your magnitude.

Not when you are of Source.

Not when you are quietly—and not so quietly—wading through illusion.

....

So, please, permit yourself to experience what your soul desires more than life itself: an illusion-free connection to everyone and everything. Immerse yourself in the centre of your being. Absorb the self-love. Radiate love. Offer empathy. Give. Know that what emanates from you will join the collective unconscious. Live this knowledge with awareness. Understand the world for what it really is. If it helps, see it as a schoolroom, movie set, dream factory or temple — whatever works to usher in greater clarity.

I realise that when you look at the state of the planet, the chaos and suffering seem real, rendering my suggestions trite at best and merciless at worst. I know it is hard to feel connected amid the cruelty and craziness. But those who are most steeped in illusion and separation are those who perpetuate insanity most. There are those who believe that causing harm to others yields no repercussions to themselves or the whole. That simply isn't true. By seeing beyond these falsities and modelling a connected way of being, ripples cast off in better directions, which the world sorely needs and with which it can join.

By steadfastly maintaining the intent to see into the truth that everything is one, you move beyond ignorance. You begin to see the unity and perfection and find yourself in a stronger position to radiate greater harmony, which will drift through humanity and contribute to healing on a planetary scale.

Far out, Blob! You're spinning me out. But I hear you. I just have one last question to help ground me. **Separation can mean a few things down here**, such as separating from a loved one. We become separated from people we care about through death and divorce. These are the things that usually spring to mind when you use the word 'separation', so would you mind elaborating on them as I rearrange my brain?

Of course, I don't mind. And you are right! The word 'separation' does indeed have different connotations, so let me delve into the meanings you mentioned according to most people's understanding.

There are times that separation seems not only real but excruciatingly painful, particularly when it comes to losing a loved one through death or the end of a relationship. On such occasions, it can feel as though your still-beating heart has been ripped from your chest. However, during these times you remain as connected to Source as ever, as do the dearly departed, as do you all to one another. Remember, your loved ones are as immortal as you are; therefore, you can only ever separate from each other physically.

While I would never dream of trivialising grief, please bear in mind that you never lose a connection to your loved one through death. Yes, you lose the tangible connection experienced through your five senses, and this hurts immensely. However, you never lose the love that was generated between you. You never disconnect from anything that you truly love. Remember, love always prevails and is the one sustainable thing within the illusion.

Therefore, by loving before, during and after the death experience, you preserve the most beautiful energy there is. Meanwhile, you and your loved one remain connected for all of eternity, for in reality, there is no death, since we are all part of the same thing and will remain so forever.

In terms of losing a hot partner, an ace job, a trustworthy friend or the many other separations that you can potentially endure, yes, these can hurt and take a long time to heal. But the real tragedy comes when you maintain your grief long past the loss and shrink away from future connections to avoid further pain.

Much of your suffering comes from the belief that you are floating around untethered, alone and unloved. The truth is you are deeply loved and connected always. The more you endeavour to realise your ongoing connection to all things, the less separation you will feel because you will come to see that separation isn't as 'real' as you think it is, no matter the guise.

I urge you to start seeing through eyes that register your connection to everything. Start with the easy stuff—the perfection of a flower, a tree or a child—then begin to appreciate the unified nature of everything. Make it your mission to notice the light wherever your gaze falls. Keep practising until you see the amalgamating energy around you in more apparent ways. It is there. It is *always* there. It is everywhere.

In closing, keep reminding yourself of who you really are. Detach from the illusion. Perceive the oneness of all things. Be kind and considerate. Love without reservation. Live fearlessly and mindfully. Strive for freedom. Be free of the false constructs of the material world that enslave you. One of the greatest gifts you will ever give yourself and the world is freedom from the erroneous concept of earthbound separation.

You are a vital part of the whole. How you interact with the people around you matters greatly. Nobody is a 'mistake' and that includes you. You are unlimited. You are vast. You are where you are for a mighty reason. You are profoundly loved. You always will be. You *are* love. You are dazzling — a stream of exquisite energy that erupted

....

from the heart of Source and from which you can never break away. *Now get out there and live like it!*

Exercise: How can you see past illusion?

This ritual helps you to see past illusion and can be done anywhere. If you've ever wondered why Source invented bladders, buses and supermarket checkouts, it's to carry out exercises like this, although it is equally effective when done in the lotus position in a dimly lit room.

Close your eyes or soften your gaze. Take three deep, replenishing breaths to settle down.

We are now going to flush clear, accurate visions of your true, higher self through your consciousness.

Here are a few examples:

You are a powerful, infinite, wondrous being who decided—for a purpose so vast and interconnected that it defies explanation—to play the game of life.

You are love.

You are light.

You are creation in motion.

You are boundless.

Keep keying these ideas into your operating system. Remember your truth and harness the power it evokes, which will assist in gently pushing past any illusion that makes you feel limited.

Then ask yourself how things would appear if you could see past the density of your illusory life. How would you feel if you saw through your shroud? Lighter? Freer? Overjoyed? Delighted? Clearer?

Whatever you feel, allow it to flow into the moment. Project it outward to bridge the gap between 'you' and 'out there'. Feel your connection to everything around you.

There is no time limit to this practice. It can run from minutes to hours. You can play with it throughout the day. The feelings it elicits can be brought into your daily life until they become second nature and you begin to see the vast interconnectedness of all things.

Cheat Sheet: Separation and Illusion

- You are divine and irrevocably connected to everyone and everything.
- You are an immense, dazzling stream of exquisite consciousness that erupted from Source, from which you can never be separated.
- You are divinity gliding through ever-changing circumstances that are no more real than a dream.
- The only sustainable reality in the dream of life is *love*.
- You are love. You are immortal. You are divine. All else is illusion.
- Living a separated existence isn't worth the pain that it causes.
- Like a drop in the ocean, you are not separate from Source or those around you.
- You are not separate from anything in the universe.
- Your ego prevents you from recognising this connection.
- The more you endeavour to experience your connection to all things, the less separated you feel.
- Ask for assistance in remembering the interconnectedness of all things.
- Live from the inside out.
- Life is but a dream.
- You were born to love.

Chapter 9. **Thought**

Dear Blob,

Whoa! That really blew my mind! In fact, it's hard to describe how the content you've provided so far has made me feel ... more energised and, dare I say, hopeful? So, thank you from the bottom of my heart for taking the time to have a yarn with me. I appreciate it more than you know.

I gather you're patiently awaiting my next question, so without any further ado, there's something that's been worrying me for some time now. It concerns my own personal 'crazy'. My thoughts are all over the shop. Sometimes they are lovely, drifty and kind, while other times they seem plucked from straight out of a horror movie!

So, how carefully should I be monitoring what runs through my mind, **or, more to the point ...**

How should I think?

Thoughtfully Yours,

The Thinker

Dear Thoughtful Thinker,

Such a well-thought-out question! Let's dive right in.

I don't know if you will take this as good or bad news, but the rumours are true: your thoughts shape your reality, so the more you cultivate ideas of separation, the more division will show up in your life. The more you focus on connection, the more you will experience oneness. If you think sparkly, beautiful thoughts, you will know a world of beauty. If you think gnarly, dark thoughts, it's the same deal.

The Universe always reflects back to you what you are thinking. That's just how it works. When you accept this and take responsibility for your life, you will find yourself in a stronger position to bring

....

greater experiences into being.

What do you mean by that? How do my thoughts shape my life?

I will preface my answer with a reminder that your reality is not as 'real' or fixed as you think. It is dreamlike, and you are both the dream and the dreamer. You orchestrate the people and circumstances in your personal universe according to what you believe. If you don't like what you see, the first thing to address is your thoughts.

Let me ask you this. For the most part, are your thoughts good, bad, loving or unloving? Are they steeped in goodwill or self-gratification? Are they aimed at understanding others or condemning them? To where does your mind drift during your downtime?

Now, let me answer on your behalf! You usually dwell upon things that perpetuate anxiety and fear: 'It's not fair!'; 'They let me down.'; 'Nobody loves me.'; 'I shouldn't be treated this way.'; 'I shouldn't be in this much pain.'; 'He's going to leave me.'; 'My boss is an armhole.' Sound familiar?

Never underestimate how much your thoughts impact your life when they are negative or doubtful. Forgive me for saying this, but from your ill-disciplined mind spills a never-ending deluge of self-sabotage and limitation, and your deep-seated beliefs play a huge role in thwarting your progress.

I, therefore, recommend that you pay closer attention to your thoughts as you move through your day. Watch them leap around like frogs on acid, deeming what's good, bad and ugly; flitting to the future with fears of decaying lily pads; hopping to the past to reflect on the great fly shortage of 2015.

When you notice your thoughts bouncing around, ask yourself

....

if expending so much energy on low-level ideas is how you'd like to spend your time. Do you really want to place your awareness in the bowels of your brain? Is it really how you'd like to exercise the immense power at your disposal when it comes to designing your life? I didn't think so. You are *way* too good for that. And your life is far too precious.

It can be a real turning point when you realise how pointless and limiting your negative thoughts are. You can start thinking more consciously and ushering in the bigger You to help steer you in better directions, aiming for the skies instead of the sewer. Doors open and close pursuant to your thoughts, so if you are thinking golden, resonant ideas, golden pathways are more likely to be revealed full of promise and wonder. And therein lies your power. Nobody can control the thoughts that you choose, only you, which makes you the master of your domain.

Thanks, Blob. So, my thoughts shape my reality. What a scary prospect! **How does it work?**

Great question, my dear!

Visualise yourself having a thought now. See yourself sitting there, thinking away and your thoughts emerging from you as 'things', perhaps as bubbles, ripples or waves. Imagine them generating in your brain and moving beyond you.

More than a concept, this is how it appears to us up here when you think. Each thought reverberates from you into the cosmos and keeps moving. That means your thoughts are incredibly important. It is for this reason that I recommend you choose what you throw into the universe carefully — trashy non-biodegradable thoughts or those closer to rose petals.

....

Another thing I would like you to imagine is a higher plane of existence that receives your thoughts. Once your desires, hopes, dreams, beliefs and ramblings are collected on this plane, wheels click into motion that bring into being the physical representations of what you have thought, which adds credence to the expression 'as above, so below'.

The image that you currently have of yourself is up here right now. Who you think you are and what you believe your life to be is being supercharged by your thoughts as we speak — either 'positively' or 'negatively'. If you continually return your consciousness to the idea that you deserve a life full of wonder, then 'wonder' will be activated and come to be in your world.

I realise that this is another of my 'out there' explanations. However, take it from me. Your thoughts are energetic. They contribute to the creation of your life and world. You are literally making things up as you go along. You hold the artist's brush and, therefore, wield the power. Call this what you like: visualisation, alchemy, daydreaming, wishful thinking or manifestation, but calling ideas of a higher vibration to mind means bringing things of a higher vibration to *life*. This equally applies to focusing on things of a lower vibration.

But please don't shudder, little one. This is great news! There is no need to wage war against your brain. Simply float above the banality of your usual chatter and tune into your most profound and magnificent thoughts. Trust me, *you can do this*. You *can* think higher thoughts, and you are more than capable of dwelling on things that can illuminate your world.

So, do your best to wrap your head around the idea that your thoughts are alive. They create. They attract. They are magnetic. They either add to or detract from the harmony of your own personal universe and the planet. They are as precious as they are dangerous, so there is no room for clumsiness when it comes to your thinking anymore.

Jeez, Blob. You're reminding me of a psychologist I once saw who tried to train me to be more aware of my thoughts. Back then my negative musings had me pinned up against a wall even before I knew I'd been thinking. I'll therefore say now what I said to him then: **controlling my thoughts is easier said than done!**

Sorry to contradict you, my love, but what I am proposing is nowhere near as daunting as you think (if you'll pardon the pun). Thought awareness is doable and can come as naturally to you as breathing.

What if you and I were to make a deal right now where you vowed to focus more on thoughts of love, security, peace, wonder and your inherent splendour? Being that we've already established that your thoughts are active, creative, potent, and shaping the content of your life, such a prospect must surely be appealing to you. And being that you have the potential to draw more tranquillity, freedom and laughter into your life by simply thinking about them, isn't that tempting? That is all I am suggesting — that you consciously heighten your thoughts and exercise discipline.

If that feels too tricky, you can always call upon the enormous energy at your disposal to aid you in your quest. As you know, universal forces, including yours truly, are always poised to help you realise your greatest potential. We are as readily available to you as your inherent power.

However, your first step in changing the way you think is to think higher thoughts. Put them out there! Believe me, you *can* think in better ways. I know you doubt me because you attempted

....

to 'change your mind' in the past and it proved difficult. As far as you were concerned, it would have been more preferable to have snapped your fingers and had your thought patterns magically realign.

All I can say to that is:

(a) You *can* change your mind, your thoughts, your brain;

(b) You can, you can, you can!

(c) You have done so in the past, more than you give yourself credit for; and

(d) Enough is enough!

Enough with the focus on how hard it is to think clearly. *Enough* with the focus on how mediocre everything and everyone is. I love you so much, but your negative thoughts have even come close to doing *my* head in, and I don't even have one! So, let's turn things around.

The reality of thoughts attracting like-energy applies to you as much as it does to everyone. Every individual is creating nonstop with his or her thoughts, all the time, everywhere, and you are in a position to add to the overall 'positivity' or 'negativity' that is shaping your planet on a global scale.

Every negative thought you have adds to the denseness of today's group consciousness, which keeps you and everyone else mired where you are. So, for the world's sake, as well as your own, please think carefully. The process of exerting mental energy in an informed, conscious way has never been more crucial. So, if nothing else, *try*!

If you need further convincing, let me remind you that whatever you focus on becomes more strongly ingrained *in you*. So, if you're thinking harshly about somebody else, feeling smug or superior, you're damaging *yourself* more than you know. We on the other side regard negative thoughts aimed at others as the psychic equivalent of smoking. Sure, passive smokers are harmed in the process, but nowhere near as much as the smokers themselves.

As I said in the last chapter, there is no separation between you and the next person. When you judge another, you judge yourself. Your higher awareness doesn't recognise the distinction between 'you' and 'them'. It experiences everything as one because everything *is* one. In simpler terms, focusing on another's shortcomings make your own more prominent. The same applies to focusing on others' luminosity. I know which one I'd choose.

That's all fine and dandy where you are, Blob, but you're not down here living life, negotiating the day-to-day grind — the work, the phone calls, the traffic, the bills, the rubbish, the hormones, the terrorists, the pandemics, the toilet cleaning, the ever-diminishing humility. **If you think it's easy to think happy thoughts, then you're more deluded than I am!**

Sweetheart, I understand what you're saying — that it's easy for me to casually dispense my infinite wisdom from a space where harmony reigns. I totally get that what you focus on in your world seems edgy and real and that many things seem to warrant negative commentary. I know that the earth experience can seem arduous and that there are deplorable circumstances from which it seems impossible to 'turn a blind eye'.

But I also know that you can either hook into life's shortcomings (and that of others) or the giddy heights of your boundlessness (and that of others). For example, you might be fixated on the injustice of having received a speeding fine until a puppy leaps onto your lap, takes a clumsy swipe and then topples over. In this instance, your thoughts become overridden with sunshine and lollipops, my point being that you feel differently according to where you cast your mind.

I realise that this is a preposterously trivial example, but I use it to illustrate a point. Whatever you place in the foreground becomes your focus, and it isn't as impossible to shift your lens as you think.

At this juncture, I would like to remind you that you are an incredible, unlimited spirit having a human experience ('cause that's just what I do), so try to remember this as you observe your musings. Also, try to observe what's happening around you from a grand perspective rather than a limited one, remembering that whatever you focus on will feel mighty real.

If you believe you cannot change your circumstances because what's occurring in your life is 'just how things are', you won't change your circumstances because what's occurring in your life is 'just how things are' pursuant to your beliefs. What you believe at a deep level will manifest as 'true'. Your wish is your command.

So, the next time I catch myself thinking negatively,
what should I do?

Immediately overlay your negative thoughts with higher ones that better align with who you really are. Also, bear in mind that positive thoughts trump negative ones, plus it never hurts to ask for an improved way of thinking or perfected belief system by calling upon Source for assistance.

I think you will agree that up to this point you have been creating your life like a half-drunk wizard with your face sliding down a wall. That's because you've been creating unconsciously and drawing on your past for inspiration, hence similar situations repeating themselves in the hope that you will learn from them and

....

move on. You have drawn in various characters playing identical roles while typecasting yourself in the same role you've played for most of your life. Whether consciously or unconsciously, you have been putting your order in with the universe and requesting the same menu item each time.

You have also looked to the external world for validation and believed in what you have seen. 'Things are what they are.' 'My circumstances are unchangeable.' 'Things are out of my control.' 'Everything is screwed.' These are incorrect assumptions steeped in illusion. They keep you stuck. If you'd care to flip from negative to positive and dedicate as much energy to your inner world as your outer, you would find yourself in a much better place.

I think I understand, but **can I get you to go over it one more time?** Given that my thoughts are moulding my life, this seems pretty important!

No problemo, friend! It *is* important.

When it comes to your thoughts, what you believe is what you get. What your mind continually feasts on is what shapes your life. What you think you deserve, you will receive. What you focus on and believe in, you will manifest. If you're wondering what you think you deserve, take stock of your life as it stands, and there you have it.

Wherever you are is a snapshot of what you have created, and what you regard as less than desirable is a clue that points to what you should examine, improve, surrender and/or change. Your outer picture shows you where to dig deeper to evolve, if not break free entirely.

Are you feeling balanced despite the turmoil of the fractious, illusory world? Are you immersed in expressions of love and peace?

....

125

Do you feel safe, secure, respected, loving, loved, elated, invigorated, stimulated, steady and free? Have you worked through your 'stuff' enough to allow yourself to live in the light? Are you injecting uplifting thoughts into the world pursuant to your soul's desires? How fortunate are you to be where you are now?

I hope that our talk today will inspire you to keep calling uplifting thoughts to mind. Remember that everything initially comes into being on your planet through thought, and what the world needs now is love, sweet love, which is why I'm pushing for you to think from the heart and the highest perspective you can. Like never before, Earth needs a healthy wave of positive thinking to usher in a more harmonious picture. Never forget that what you think literally contributes to the direction in which you all head. *Every thought counts.*

To finish up, what you focus on comes to life, so keep your thoughts high. Keep calling to mind what you already have and add a flourish of gratitude. Keep calling to mind who you want to be. Think positive thoughts. Brand them onto your brain. Tame the mind. Revisit visions of all things good. Picture how an enlightened life might look. Envision how it might feel to live in a peaceful world. Supercharge your desires with God-consciousness. Feel them in the most sensory way that you can. See your superfluous, heavy thoughts dropping away. Be optimistic. Broadcast love. Absorb the enormous beauty that abounds. Reflect on all that is virtuous. Think compassionately. Monitor what you're putting 'out there'. Be diligent and aware. Will good for all. And strive for what you want in the physical world through being motivated by Source.

If you continue to think dazzling thoughts, mighty things will come to pass, and a being of your eminence deserves nothing less.

You are so naïve in respect to your personal power that I just want to squeeze you!

....

Exercise: How can you change your thinking?

What you focus on is what you get, which can be a scary prospect considering the time spent dwelling on what you *don't* want.

Today's experiment involves spending the day living as though you have no issues whatsoever in your life, that everything is, 'Just fabulous, thank you very much. Please pass me the maple syrup.'

This suggestion may stir resistance in you along the lines of, 'Yes, that's all well and good, but I don't earn enough money, I've been hustled again, my Internet is down, and I still have ugly feet!'

If that is the case, try laying that aside for a while, remembering that you have been keeping what you *don't* want at centre stage for much of your life, so you are entitled to problem-free thinking for just one tiny day. Things will continue to chug along as they normally would while you place your awareness on more liberating ideas.

Call to mind all that is good in your world. Imagine your life oozing with peace, love and light. Keep reminding yourself as often as you can:

Today is a problem-free day.

Cheat Sheet: Thought

- Your thoughts create your reality.
- Your thoughts are energetic.
- Your life is a snapshot of your thoughts and beliefs.
- What you imagine you will experience.
- Ideas of a higher vibration bring things of a higher vibration to life.
- People and circumstances manifest according to your beliefs.
- Thinking ill of others hurts *you* more than it hurts them.
- You *can* change your thoughts.
- You *can* shift your focus.
- There is a higher plane of existence that receives your thoughts.
- The Universe dispenses a vibrational match to your thought energy.
- Your mind is powerful and requires constant discipline.
- Positive thoughts trump negative ones.
- Overlay negative thoughts with positive ones.
- Focus on love, security, peace, wonder and your inherent splendour.
- Draw in more serenity, tranquillity, freedom and laughter.
- Only *you* can control your thought-focus.
- You are the creator of your world.
- Thoughts shape your planet.
- Conscious thinking has never been more imperative.
- You deserve good.
- The world deserves good.
- Will good for all.
- Be grateful.
- Be positive.
- Be compassionate.

- You were born to love.

Chapter 10. *Manifestation*

....
130

Dear Blob,

I feel slightly sheepish going where I'm about to go, but I noticed you alluded to manifestation back there, which is a subject I've been both fascinated with and frustrated by for years. I think I understand the concept well enough, but I've never really managed to 'create' anything of lasting significance, so my next question is ...

Can I really create 'stuff' using my mind?

To be clear, I'm not asking this because I'm a superficial, money-grubbing, materialistic buffoon.

Cordially Yours,

Humble Fragment of the Multiverse

Dear sweet little fragment that I would never in a million years describe as a superficial, money-grubbing, materialistic buffoon.

Manifestation, huh? It is indeed a fascinating subject that nicely rolls off the back of our last discussion, and I'm glad you've asked about it because you've had me in stitches in the past, like the time you attempted to manifest a cat through sheer thought-power alone. Remember that?

We blobs couldn't believe our 'eyes' when you followed the instructions of a manifestation documentary and printed out a picture of a cat's face, stuck it to a rolled up cardigan and stroked it whenever you sat on the sofa watching television, the idea being to act as though you already had what you wanted. We still chuckle over that one to this day, so please allow me the luxury of another quick guffaw before we begin!

Also, thank you for highlighting that you are not a 'money-grubbing buffoon'. This saves me the agony of instructing you on how to conjure up a fleet of private jets or magical trips to Paris where you share a baguette with *the* perfect lover as you both gnaw on opposite ends of a breadstick till you meet halfway, gaze into each other's eyes and fall into a kiss.

If you are anything like me—and I'd suggest you are, only I'm wobblier, blurrier and for the most part invisible—then a bittersweet taste may have been left in your mouth with respect to the commercialised version of manifestation that sprang to life a while ago complete with bells, whistles and a complimentary pair of jazz hands. Still, the power of intention is one of the coolest tools at your disposal. *And it works.*

A tonne has already been written on this subject, but the mainstream emphasis has generally been on conjuring up things of a materialistic persuasion, which tends to keep people ego-bound and focused on separated ways of living. Yes, you can manifest money, clients, jobs, partners, racehorses and attractive biceps, but manifestation can be used much more meaningfully.

I highlight this owing to the much-touted concept that if you pay enough attention to the external world and exert every ounce of energy you have toward putting everything in place—the perfect body, career, relationship, bank balance, car, house, teeth, status, KPIs, web hits, *cat*—then everything will be fine. The restlessness within will subside, and all will be well.

I mean, *come on!* Think about it! Do you *really* believe that? Does anybody? Have you ever known your ego to be satisfied, for you to reach a goal, dust off your hands, and say, 'Okay, we're all done here. I'm completely appeased, and all is in order'? No. It doesn't work like that. It's usually more a case of, 'Is that it?', 'What's next?' or 'I'd have preferred it in black.'

The tiny flaw in attempting to manifest external desires is that nothing external is as real or permanent as you think. Even if everything did miraculously fall into place, your circumstances could change on a dime. It's happened often enough. You and I both know that there is no great permanency to anything in the external world, which again affords me the opportunity to remind you of two of my favourite things:

Your world is illusory.

And:

That which you seek is within.

For the love of Blob, stop yawning! It may be old news, but *it's true*!

Of course, the ego will never accept this. In fact, I just heard it groan from all the way up here! It will never accept an ongoing state of contentment. To do so would mean it relinquishing control. Long-term gratification will therefore forever be elusive pursuant to its investment in the idea that you are separated from everything, including that which you seek.

The good news is that you and your spirit are never apart from anything, and your spirit is incredibly vigilant in capitalising on opportunities that are far richer than anything your ego could conceive. Your spirit can help you to see past the fleetingness of your day-to-day desires, for it is consistent, enduring and reliable. Your ego is not. It is through the cultivation of the former that you will be free of fear and in a position to create exactly what you want ... which may not be what you think you want right now.

Eventually you will arrive at the point of appreciating the perfection of everything, no matter what is going on in your world, no matter what you do or don't have, and no matter what improvements you believe need to be made. You will see Source in all things, meaning materialistic matters will take their rightful place.

Through concentrating on your inner power and the essence of your desires, you will begin to notice the shadows of your life shifting and changing without buying into their validity. There will no longer be days where you feel invincible and others where you feel weak because you will realise that your ups and downs are perpetuated by the world's stage (with the ego playing director), and that you are spiritually poised regardless.

With all this in mind, the type of manifestation I recommend involves you fostering a steady sense of spiritual empowerment. By engaging your inner power, you are quite literally unstoppable and on the path to experiencing consistent contentment. And at the end of the day, isn't that what it's all about?

I guess so, but I'll be honest here, Blob. **I want the spiritual stuff for sure.** But I want other stuff, too. Is that wrong?
Can't I have both?

Well, I understand that you'd like a few other things in your life, like your own home and a non-moulting, toilet-trained kitty, and these are certainly attainable. But when it comes to manifesting the life of your dreams, I hold steadfast that this should be approached *spiritually*. Therefore, the number one question you should always ask before attempting to bring anything into being is: *What does this thing that I want represent?*

Using our earlier examples of a fleet of jets, a baguette-lover in Paris, owning your own home and cat, I would propose that these things represent a wish for *greater love and security*. See what I did there? I drilled down to determine what is *really* wanted at a much deeper level.

To provide another example, let's say you desire a red sports car. This might be because you'd really like to feel more abundant, unique, alive and free. If you steadily focus on the *feelings* associated with your wishes, physical representations that match your desires will arise as a matter of course. You will know that you are on track when the counterparts of your wishes show up, whether in the form of a sports car or not.

I am suggesting that you crave *feelings* more than you do *things*. I really hope you can hear me on this, as it's rather important, as is manifestation's key principle, which is: *That which you concentrate on is made manifest.*

Therefore, to concentrate on, say, a lump of red metal on wheels can curb a greater outcome that exceeds matter, and exerting all your energy on solely manifesting a car kind of borders on lunacy ... or it does according to my bulbous, enlightened mind, anyway!

So, let us say you crave love, security and freedom, and perhaps other non-material things like serenity, contentment and greater insight. This is where you begin your manifestation workout, prioritising how you want to feel, working from the inside out and striving as you would with any worthwhile exercise regime.

You can still have your dreams. You can still 'have it all'. You can still create 'Heaven on Earth'. But when it comes to manifesting 'stuff', carefully consider what you would like from the highest perspective you can. How do you want to *feel* whilst living your life as opposed to what *thing* would you like to hold in your hands that you think will bring about that satisfaction? There is a huge difference, you know, so get your feelings clear before boldly bringing anything into being. Think long and hard about what you really want.

....

Sure I can!

To really set yourself free, concentrate on that which ignites your *spirit*. Think about how you'd like to feel as a spiritual being roaming the globe. Imagine your days infused with love and light, peace and wisdom, service and compassion, well-being and humility, integrity and sincerity, insightfulness and a heightened state of awareness.

Maybe you'd like to experience greater self-love, fearlessness, contentment, joy, grace, safety, happiness and wellness. Perhaps you'd like to feel more caring, giving, knowledgeable and awakened. Maybe you'd like to be more openhearted, free, gentle, caring, comforted, inspired, satisfied, connected, prosperous, balanced and nurturing, or more aware and attuned to your godliness, perfection, power, opulence, purity, innocence, beauty, boundlessness, divinity, and that of everyone else. Maybe you'd like to live on purpose and love life.

If you wish to go placidly amid the haste and tread lightly upon the earth; if you hope to be spiritual yet of the world; if you hope to touch others' lives — to shed your fears, connect with Source, enjoy nature, appreciate people, increase your joy and be steeped in serenity, these are the images and feelings to hold on high!

These are the sensations to rehash all day, every day. This is what you return to in your mind's eye over and over again. This is the yearning you carry in your heart as you go about your business. This is what you act upon in your daily life. This is what you know you deserve. This is what you shoot for as you discard denser energies and ascend higher.

Don't go all dreamy over the circumstances you believe will

....

bring these things into being, just dwell on the feelings themselves. Be anticipatory because they are well within your grasp. You are absolutely capable of bringing them and their associated circumstances to fruition. And, again, it has less to do with *things* than you think.

If you choose this trajectory, you will absolutely, unequivocally and definitely co-create a higher reality in collaboration with Source. Physical manifestations that match your energy will line up like ducks — you wait and see! Focusing on sensations of a divine nature will allow your spirit to flourish and, as you know, I can't spruik these benefits enough. Keep flicking the switch till you are permanently 'on'. Pull your focus from the external world to your inner world and feel the power surging through you.

If you wish to experience that power more, be very clear about it. *Acknowledge* your potency. *Decide* how you would like to feel. *Affirm* it. *Say* it aloud ... unless you happen to be in the fresh food aisle of the supermarket! Then feel, listen and act while looking out for signs of what you are cultivating. Call your wishes to mind constantly. Be vigilant.

Picture yourself embodying your desires as clearly as you can. Imagine living your life as this new version of you. Stay with it until you feel a subtle shift. When you sense that tiny click, it means the wheels are in motion. I know you felt something moving inside you simply through me rattling off suggestions. That movement is *it*. If you can embody how the words make you feel, physical representations will follow.

Divine connection is at the pinnacle of your soul-driven aspirations. With this in mind, it makes sense to reach skyward and build your days around exploring the heights of your human experience; to set your intentions high and be the best version of yourself that you can; to strive for what you want with utter conviction; to remind yourself that you want to be filled by the light.

....

Yes, there are never-ending experiences available to you while you are in human form. You can parachute from a plane, be pummelled by waves, writhe with a lover, but at the zenith of your cravings is the desire to experience your sweet divinity. There is no greater high. And, trust me, I wouldn't be promoting it with such vigour if I knew of anything greater.

Alright, but to draw you back down to Earth for a minute, **what if I accidentally think negatively**, which I do all the time? Will that weigh me down?

In a nutshell, yes. But if you catch yourself ruminating over how you *don't* want to feel, stop! Drop into your awareness and evoke your preferred feelings instead. Remember, positive thoughts trump negative ones, and you are a powerful being. You can bring amazing things to life, so stay aware and gently correct any negative thoughts with positive ones that are better aligned with who you really are.

Reach out to the bigger, light-filled You to help heighten your thinking. Redirect your neural traffic. Stay on course. Positively create with a view to bursting free of illusion. Ask us for help! Combine your conscious mind and spiritual desires with our assistance to bring about what you want and watch an amazing world bloom around you as though you are thriving in an exquisite piece of art. Search for every available opportunity to experience what you hope to. Live your highest good.

Focus on wisdom, courage, love, illumination and tapping directly into the divine essence of who you are. So many breathtaking circumstances await you, so keep your ideals high and go within to play the most exciting conjuring game of all time.

Now is the time to capitalise on all opportunities. Be vigilant

....

for anything aligned with your wishes. *Live* the greater self-love, fearlessness, contentment, laughter, freedom, peace, compassion, lightness, safety, happiness, wellness, well-being and love. *Be* more caring, giving, knowing, awakened, openhearted, gentle, comforting, comforted, inspired, happy, satisfied, inspirational, connected, prosperous, balanced and nurturing. *Be* more spiritually attuned to your godliness, perfection, power, opulence, purity, innocence, beauty, boundlessness, divinity and luminousness.

Think long and hard about what you want spiritually and what you believe you deserve. Fold in some clarity, add a splash of excitement and envision the most vivid, harmonious and wondrous life you can, replete with the essence of soul growth and sweetness. It's time to get cooking!

Thanks for the culinary motivation, Blob, but like I said before, I've tried to manifest a better life in the past and it hasn't quite worked. **Where did I go wrong?**

That's what I've been trying to tell you! You focussed on *objects* and specific outcomes.

From now on, stick to the magic formula. Think about how you would like to *feel*. Check that it aligns with what you believe you deserve. If it does, *persist, expect and act. Be open to receive.* That's all there is to it!

These steps are as relevant to becoming financially abundant as they are to becoming enlightened. If you believe in financial ease, ease can be yours. If you believe in enlightenment, enlightenment can be yours, and I will have much more to say on this matter later on.

In the meantime, if you aren't receiving what you are putting out there, ask whether others have experienced what you hope to

. . . .

139

yourself. Chances are they have, and so you can too. One of the main reasons you don't have what you think you want is because you believe it's beyond your reach and exceeds what you deserve. If you think you don't deserve something, ask yourself why and begin to replace your limiting ideas with the truth — *that you deserve all that is good.* I'll repeat that because I noticed you flinched: *You deserve all that is good.* You really do!

Another point I would like to raise is if you've tried and tried again to bring something into being, there is a chance you have already experienced it in another form and your soul has no need for it again, or your soul has no need for it at all, or your growth is coming by way of you *not* having what you think you want for the sake of instilling acceptance or patience.

It is cute that you desire a perfectly aligned illusion 100 per cent of the time, or that you strive for the same stuff lifetime after lifetime. But I suggest that you go for something slightly more exotic this time around, like awakening from the dream, which is far less fleeting than being draped across a chaise lounge and being fed grapes!

If you can acknowledge that everything is aligned with your soul's requirements for the sake of your evolution—even when life doesn't seem as crash hot as you'd like it to be—then your ability to accept the precision of everything will lead to transformation. By accepting that *all is as it should be*, you will begin to register that everything is poised for your enlightenment always, whether you have this, that or the other, or not.

Nothing needs to be skewed to the left or right for you to embody God. This is big stuff that I hope to expand upon in another of our thrilling instalments, but I long for the day that you will see that you are in the perfect situation *right now* to leap out of the illusion. All that is required is that you open your mind.

Before I sign off, I touched on treading lightly upon the earth earlier, so let us spare a thought for your gorgeous planet. When you consider how you would like to feel, may I humbly request that you keep the earth in mind too? Have a think about its enormity, intensity and beauty; how miraculous and special it is; how it slowly turns with incredible reliability. Call to mind an image of it from space — so radiant, mysterious and breathtaking.

When you extract the human drama playing out upon it, the earth endures with unbelievable devotion and tranquillity. By calling this to mind, you view your globe in its purest form, devoid of all the turmoil imposed upon it by its inhabitants, or, rather, by its inhabitants' egos. By returning to this image often, you help to restore sanctity to your enchanting playground, as well as provide yourself with the perfect metaphor for your true self.

I really love you, you know. You are doing exceedingly well. You are moving further into your power, and I couldn't be prouder.

Till next time, Dear One, keep on rocking in the free world!

Exercise: How can you manifest?

Here is a simple exercise that will not only bring greater things into being, but uplift you in the process.

Consider what you would most like to embody today. Here are some menu items to choose from:

Self-love. Fearlessness. Contentment. Joy. Freedom. Gracefulness. Security. Happiness. Wellness. Compassion. Generosity. Knowledge. Openheartedness. Gentleness. Inspiration. Satisfaction. Connection. Prosperity. Balance. Nurturance. Spirituality. Awareness. Perfection. Power. Opulence. Purity. Innocence. Beauty. Boundlessness. Divinity. Luminousness. Purposefulness. Peacefulness. Serenity. Awakening. Love.

Now ...

- **Choose** what you would like to embody.
- **Focus** on it.
- **Feel** it.
- **Ensure** that it aligns with your beliefs.
- **Ask** for its prominence in your life.
- **Anticipate** it; be excited; know that it's here.
- **Act** on any opportunities that allow it to flourish more in your life.

When I say 'focus', I mean *really* focus on it, not in a New Year's resolution kind of way where come January 2 you are found with chocolate and a guilty smirk smeared across your face! This is about enduring effort.

When I say 'feel', I mean *really* feel yourself embodying your chosen way of being. Sense mysterious and miraculous energy shining through any fissures of doubt.

In many ways, your life is already awesome, yet it could be even better. So dare to dabble and have a blast while you're at it. Your life is a divine adventure, so enjoy it to the hilt.

Cheat Sheet: Manifestation

- Manifestation works.
- It is one of the coolest tools at your disposal.
- That which you focus on is made manifest.
- Materialistic goals are often ego-based and promote separated, limited living.
- Altruistic desires point to your soul cravings.
- Create what ignites your spirit.
- Capitalise on opportunities that bypass fleeting desires.
- Your spirit is consistent, enduring and reliable.
- Your ego isn't.
- Your ego wants 'stuff'.
- The ego will never be satisfied.
- The ego will never accept enduring contentment.
- Nothing external will deliver everlasting satisfaction.
- What you seek is within.
- Prioritise how you would like to feel while rocking the planet.
- Feel your way into higher states of being.
- Create from the highest perspective you can.
- Focus on the greatest traits that you wish to embody.
- Get clear about what you want, expect it, act on it and be open to receive.
- All is as it should be.
- You were born to love.

Chapter 11. **Invocation**

Dearest Blob,

You have recommended more than once that I enlist the help of those in your stratosphere as I forge ahead. **Correct me if I'm wrong, but are you suggesting I pray?**

If you are, then that scares me a bit because (a) a lot of people down here don't do that anymore; (b) many believe it's silly, old-fashioned and weird, if not delusional; and (c) whenever I've done it, I've never noticed any real intercession when it's come to my prayers being answered.

Also, on the odd occasion that I have taken to bended knee, I am mortified to think that you have seen me coughing and spluttering as I've begged the high heavens to come to my aid.

My official question is, though ... Is prayer a big, fat waste of time?

Apologies for being so blunt, but I'm that kind of cat.

Kindest regards,

Curious Resident of the Universe

Dear Curious Cat,

You are so cute!

In short, the answer is *no*, prayer is *not* a big, fat waste of time, but you were expecting me to say that, right?

You were also hoping that I would assuage your fears over me having seen you cry to the heavens with mucus evacuating from your nostrils at alarming speeds. The answer to that one, I'm afraid, is *yes*,

....

I *have* seen that, *a lot*, but on those occasions, I inflated with so much love, compassion and empathy that other blobs began parading me around like an enormous novelty balloon!

So, yes, I have witnessed you turning a brighter shade of beetroot and bursting all known capillaries as you have screamed out for a reprieve from God. But I have also applauded you for asking for help. You are actually quite adept at requesting assistance during your hours of need, so perhaps you are not as opposed to prayer as you think you are. However, might I suggest that you pray outside your times of turmoil as well?

I know what you're about to say, so I will save you the breath. You are *way* too busy for regular prayer as you flit from one thing to the next. In fact, so trapped are you in your so-called reality that even the *concept* of praying seems antiquated and the opposite of 'cool'.

But, I will say this as clearly as I can. Whenever you cry out for help, blessings, comfort, healing or courage, you are heard every single time. You are *never* ignored. Source is always present. There is always movement in response to your pleas.

This is because a creative process begins when you pray, whereby an energetic match is drawn to your requests in the form of comfort, guidance and support. It therefore makes sense to heighten your vibration and surrender more often than you do, knowing that unseen forces are responding whether you are in the throes of catastrophe or not.

Also, if you really stop to think about it, there are multiple examples of your prayers having been answered, perhaps not as instantaneously as you would have liked, but things have shifted nonetheless.

It is truly wondrous!

Even though prayer has had its function watered down over the ages, and some regard it as a 'big, fat waste of time' [*wink*], it remains one of *the* most powerful and misunderstood systems available to humankind.

Prayer is a blessed form of communication through which you can demonstrate your humility over being a *part* of the universe, rather than the *centre* of it. You can call in help for others, express gratitude and bolster a positive focus on what you have, as well as request improvements. It is a means of offering and acquiring blessings, protection and healing; a channel through which you can commune with mighty light-filled energies as though having an intimate conversation with a close friend. It is a means of demonstrating reverence for the Source of All Things.

So, whenever you get down 'on bended knee', as you put it, you are showing your willingness to surrender to something infinitely vaster than your ego and bridging the gap between yourself and your Self. You are tapping into the unlimited power of the Universe and opening yourself up for guidance, peace, connection and lucidity. You are quietening the mind and anchoring to the now.

Prayer also helps to facilitate your intentions. If intention is a seed hopeful of one day blossoming into a mighty oak tree, then prayer is its watering. It calls in the ideal conditions for your desires to come to fruition. Therefore, it is not restricted to a verbal exercise with your hands clasped at your chest. It is a far cry from, 'Dear God, I know we haven't spoken in a while but ...' It isn't, 'If you do this, I'll do that.' It isn't a babble of words gabbled by rote without thought for their meaning. It isn't braying your demands to the heavens before cyber-stalking your ex! Genuine, heartfelt prayer is nothing like that at all. Rather, it is humble, reverent, pure, patient and potent, and another means of assisting you to live the best life you can.

Unlike the concept of crying into the darkness in the wild hope of a deity charging in to save the day, or praying to insure against fire and brimstone, or 'being good' to curry favour, prayer is a gentle practice that beckons higher energies closer while purifying your energy field. There is an enormous difference between bona fide prayer and your ego shrieking out its wants and demands, having a hissy fit, chucking a tantrum and crying out like an entitled baby.

'Prayer', as styled by the ego, is conditional and devoid of surrender. It is loaded with fear. It is based on wants with little regard for consequences, and it usually insists upon instant gratification. Remember, the ego is only ever interested in surface-level stuff — for things to change to better suit its alleged needs; for the jigsaw puzzle pieces to be cut with scissors and forced into place.

Praying for people to change, or to love you, or to win the lottery, cheat death or exact revenge is the antithesis of what prayer is about. Yes, you can pray for the circumstances of your life and everyone else's to be blessed and on target for the greater good of all, but you cannot bargain for intervention in what is already in motion to bring about growth. You cannot expect an almighty god to step in to do your bidding. And you cannot pretend to know what soul purpose lies behind the seemingly undesirable situations that you find yourselves in.

Source does not alter the course of that which is for the highest good. Circumstances designed for growth often make little sense at the time, I know. But from the grandest perspective there is, everything is always playing out as it should.

So, if you misperceive prayer as a means of changing the course of your destiny or anyone else's, it runs the risk of you 'failing', Source 'failing' you, and you feeling 'unheard' all over again.

Okay. But back to your point that everything is always playing out as it should, **I'll bear that in mind the next time a terrorist mows down a bunch of innocent bystanders or we're all forced into lockdown**. Oh, sorry! Did I think that out loud? But do you know what I mean? **If I can't use prayer to change what I'd like to, then what can I pray for?**

Everything, especially people who mow down innocent bystanders, as well as the innocent bystanders themselves! And especially for the expeditious healing of the planet.

When it comes to how prayer is most frequently used, let's just say a lot of airtime is taken up with personal desires. But one can also pray for others, that they are evolving and making the most of their incarnations. You can pray for peace, the world, humanity and the illumination of your fellows. You can offer blessings to whomever you choose. You can give thanks to God. You can pray in concert with others, adding to the global broadcast that is received up here as a symphony of light.

And, before you ask, *yes, yes, yes*, you can pray for yourself. You can express gratitude for all that you have. You can put forward your spiritually motivated desires. You can pray for forgiveness and the strength to forgive. You can pray for the courage to move through what is before you. You can pray for awakening, the health of your mind, body and spirit, for growth, surrender, grace, humility and wisdom. You can pray for *anything* with the highest intentions you have.

At this juncture, have a little think about what you would like to pray for. Now, tell me what you want, what you really, really want.

. . . .

Do you want peace, healing and protection for your glorious planet? Do you want greater radiance so that you may better serve those around you and be more spiritually alive? Do you want to live a life of excellence? To feel more bolstered by the Divine? To exude greater serenity and strength? To be emotionally balanced? To experience greater insight, vaster awareness, expanded consciousness and metaphysical excitement? Do you want to send blessings to your friends, family, strangers and nature? Or would you like to accept your lessons and evolve so that you may enjoy an improved life? Then be bold and *ask* for it!

Regularly request expansion for yourself and your contemporaries. Ask to move farther into the layers of light as your miraculous life unfolds. Ask for help with making the most of your existence, living on purpose and achieving what you have set out to do. Have the 'audacity' to ask for more love.

See yourself as we do, as a strong beacon. When you pray, your brightness intensifies. The more you do it, the greater the radiance. You are a precious beam within an ever-expanding universe. You are in a magnificent position to send out a continuous broadcast that says, 'I want to make the most of this life. I want to give love. I want to receive love. I want to give compassion. I want to receive compassion. I want to give peace. I want to receive peace. I want to give joy. I want to receive joy. I want to be of service. I want to experience my spiritual self. Please help me, help me, help me!'

You can express prayers like these continually. They aren't restricted to a couple of minutes before bedtime, only to be forgotten in the morning. Give praise, send blessings, request your soul-motivated desires and move through the world with your prayers in your heart, ensuring that there is always a piece of you dialled into Source.

If you find yourself struggling at certain times of the day, do more than shake your fist at the sky. Ask for help in ascertaining

....

what's the nub of your lesson. Are you being steered toward greater love, peace, forgiveness, learning, open-heartedness, light, delight or fearlessness? Are you being compelled to shed guilt and shame? Or are you being prompted to love yourself more?

Draw your awareness to the centre of your being—your heart—and sense the space within that is open to receive. Know that the Universe supports you. *Ask* for divine assistance. *Ask* for divine guidance. *Ask* for greater expansion. You deserve to be immersed in good, clean, positive energy, and that's what Source wants for you, too. So, don't be afraid to request it.

I know that these suggestions could be deemed fluffy if you are caught in the middle of a shi*p*-storm (see how I replaced the *t* with a *p* to conform with polite society?)! Yet I must stress that extraordinarily good things are with and around you whether you realise it or not, believe it or not, feel heard or not, or do or don't pray.

Prayer is you plugging into the motherboard and grasping the myriad of invisible hands that are forever outstretched to support you.

I will try to remember that. But I have to admit that **shouting out to the invisible sounds a tad whimsical.**

Whimsical? Good Lord! While I may have intimated that some of my suggestions risk sounding fluffy, prayer is far from whimsical. The receiving Universe is incredibly precise! It is alive with vital energy that thrills at being summoned. It delights in infusing you and your planet with light. You are a dynamic, crackling, ready-to-be-charged receptor capable of receiving vast amounts of energy from incredible sources. These sources are in constant motion and perpetually poised, and you are invited to call upon them — every second, every breath, every day. You call, they yield, only *you don't do that*, which is a crying shame because *if this energy isn't summoned, it doesn't budge.* If you don't ask, you don't get. Remember that.

Exquisite, abundant energy surrounds you and adheres to your call. That energy knows a thing or two. In fact, it knows everything. It longs to share its wisdom. It longs to assist. It longs to resonate with your gratitude and heartfelt desires. It longs for your humility and for you to surrender so that you may be drawn higher. There are corresponding whispers to your prayers and you have ears, so listen. Don't think that by asking, you are putting anyone out. You aren't! Your call will be answered by the first available operator, of which there are many. *So ask!*

Never hesitate to ask for what is important to you as a gorgeous little creature doing your best to live out your days on planet Earth. Again, you are deeply loved by unseen forces regardless of what you think, what's going on, who you are pretending to be or what you are doing with your life. The love of Source is never withheld, but it is through prayer that you can remain consciously connected.

When you request a world full of love, peace, compassion, healing, light, delight, fearlessness and egolessness, you contribute to the strengthening of that energy. Prayer is a tender means of drawing more goodness into your world. It ensures that the entitled infant less directs the steeplechase of your life. Your resolve has the capacity to contribute to the greater good of all. Blockages will shift. You will be met halfway. And you will be uplifted — all of you.

So, send love and thanks to yourself and everything around you. Surrender. Venerate. And share your most intimate yearnings with the Source of All Things.

I'm about to tend to some prayer-answering now, as it happens. Any advice on how I should best address a request for a giraffe riding a penny-farthing?

．．．．．．．．．．．．

Exercise: How do you pray?

You know how to pray in your own special way. You have your private language, ritual and relationship with Source. However, if you wish for an improved life and planet, *ask for it.*

Just ask!

If you'd like more joy, *ask for it* and vigorously search for it inside your heart and out in the world. If you'd like more peace, *ask for it* and vigorously search for it in the same way.

Focus on what you want, employ grace, pray for it and surrender.

Not only is Source poised to enhance your experience, but so too are the many expressions of light that want nothing more than for you to feel what they do: moved by love and spiritual upliftment.

Openly receive what the Universe wants for you and share it. Peace, love, learning, laughter, compassion, light, delight, fearlessness, egolessness, healing and everything in between are yours for the asking, so shout it out loud, confident that divine forces are poised to help.

Cheat Sheet: Invocation

- Prayer is *not* a big, fat waste of time!
- Prayer is a powerful yet misunderstood tool available to humankind.
- Prayer is pure, potent and reverent.
- Prayer demonstrates that you are a *part* of the universe, not the centre of it.
- Prayer demonstrates that you are willing to surrender to something bigger than yourself.
- Prayer is a blessed avenue through which you can communicate with the Divine.
- Prayer is a gentle practice that beckons higher energies to draw closer.
- Prayer is an expression of humility and gratitude.
- Prayer helps to maintain a positive focus.
- Prayer bridges the gap between yourself and your Self.
- There is a difference between your ego shrieking out its demands and genuine prayer.
- The ego is only interested in surface level stuff.
- Pray during good *and* bad times.
- Send blessings to others.
- Pray for everyone's life to be on target for the greater good of all.
- Abundant energy surrounds you and is poised to help.
- This energy doesn't move unless it is summoned.
- Don't ask, don't get. So *ask*!
- Ask for more love, peace, light, delight, wisdom, learning, healing, compassion, serenity, fearlessness, egolessness, charitable opportunity and anything else in between.
- Ask for soul evolution and a vastly improved life.

....

- Ask for what you want at your deepest level and know that unseen forces will respond.
- Pray from your heart and maintain that awareness.
- You were born to love.

Chapter 12. *Emotion*

Dear Blob,

How can I ever repay you? What does one give an entity that has everything? This feels slightly one-sided—me constantly firing off questions, you answering—but it has been one of the greatest things to have ever happened to me ... and I've met Robert Smith of the Cure!

I would now like to discuss my nut-jobbery, if that's okay with you. When my emotions are at their worst, they seem beyond my control. There was even a time where death seemed preferable to the suffering they imposed, which just goes to show how intense and destructive they can feel. So ...

How do I deal with my difficult emotions?

Kindest regards,
Queen of Tempestia

Your Majesty,

The concept of you 'repaying' me for loving you is as foreign to me as being forced to do the Nutbush in pink taffeta at a wedding reception. To an advanced blob of consciousness, the gift is in the giving, and as Minnie Riperton once said, 'Lovin' you is easy 'cause you're beautiful'. But that wasn't how I intended to open this chapter.

I was planning to kick it off by saying *you have nothing to fear*. I say that because if you boil your tumultuous emotions down, they are expressions of fear and reactions to the external world. They are *not you*. And being that you are who you are—a divine, limitless being—there is nothing to be afraid of.

I offer that preface before acknowledging your difficult emotions. Without wishing to minimise the magnitude of your worth,

....

your lifespan is but a tiny pair of brackets within infinite time and space. Inside those brackets, you remain a gorgeous, melodious, vibrant and creative creature having a trippy experience within a generously abundant and altruistic universe.

But unlike on other planes of existence, on Earth you *feel*. Boy, do you feel! You can experience emotional explosions that put Mount Vesuvius to shame, and the emotional rollercoaster you ride is like no other. Unless you approach matters with the right attitude, it can be one heck of a bumpy ride where situations fly at you, your stomach pitches, you duck, weave, scream, wave your arms, battle your wits, disembark exhausted and do your best not to barf.

You were *happy* that you got to enjoy the ride, but grew *sad* when it was over. You were *scared* that your carriage might derail. You were *angry* at the ticket price, the shortness of the ride and the fact that you now have whiplash. You were *jealous* that you were ushered to the middle section rather than the front, and, as you exited the park, you felt *lonely, empty* and slightly *confused*.

On the wacky ride of life, you wig out constantly and, of course, it feels incredibly real. It is not my intention to diminish your feelings, including those related to health, wealth, career, relationships, injustices, heartbreak, existential angst and Twitter. Each of these can certainly be anxiety-provoking, but perhaps not to the degree that you allow them.

I want you to know that when difficulties arise, *it is not the circumstances that hurt you but how you respond to them*, which is the point I have been trying to reach. *You* are responsible for your own happiness. The lack of joy in your life is attributable to your reactions. You ascribe your torment to what has happened 'out there' — to the past, to how somebody wronged you, to how the world at large 'sucks'. But it is your response to such things that constitute your misery.

You try to jiggle your circumstances to make everything okay, which is understandable. But I suggest, as always, that it would be wiser to work from the inside out, search within, discover your areas of discontent and resolve them, particularly anything that proves to be a barrier to love.

I understand what you're saying, Blob, but you know how it is. Emotional assaults can seem to come from nowhere and be incredibly intense. **What should I do if I find myself terrorised by my emotions?**

If I had a body, here's where I'd don a designer suit and wireless microphone, and strut around a stage spruiking the benefits of spiritually informed emotional intelligence and go on to become a self-made millionaire. Instead, I bequeath this to you free of charge.

During times of despair, the first thing I recommend you do is remember that you are *immortal*. You never end. You are a piece of *the* ultimate energy force, which is indestructible, eternal, immense and powerful beyond measure. The moment jagged emotions take hold, remind yourself of this. Call to mind your wondrous divinity.

Remind yourself that you are a mystical being whose core vibrates with peace. No matter what's playing out in your drama, at your deepest level you are pain-free. Your inner being exists beyond the discomfort of the human experience. The amazing truth of who you really are is always present, consistent and serene, as I've mentioned many times before.

At the onset of your next calamity, do your best to bear that in mind. Allow yourself a tiny space from the tumult to recall that you are starring in a play that is taking place within an infinite, benevolent universe. This will help to return you to the bigger picture, and can be used as the foundation for overcoming your pain. And now that we have laid it, let us delve deeper.

The next thing I suggest you do is: *Breathe.*

Tune into your breath—in out, in out—and note that on some level you are okay. Your emotions aren't as all-pervading as they seem. They may be dominating you, but you still have plenty of other 'bits' that are steady and okay. Plenty of you is still vibrating in perfect symmetry. You are still alive. You are still respiring. The pain is certainly there, but it hasn't killed you.

So, your advice is essentially, 'Don't forget to breathe.' Ingenious! If you hadn't said it, I'd have surely passed out!
What else have you got?

Your sarcasm is duly noted, cheeky, but believe it or not, I do have more.

Once you have breathed, begin to exercise a healthy amount of *acceptance.* Claim your painful emotions as your own and be curious about what they have to say. I recommend this because you have a tendency to deny your emotions and be rid of them as soon as you can. You reject them. You banish them. You blame their origins on external forces. But while your unwanted feelings may appear to be the result of something that's happened 'out there', they have come from *you.* They are your emotional offspring, so pay attention to them, nurture them and accept them as you might accept your own children, birth defects and all.

Celebrate your less-than-perfect parts when they make themselves known. Throw a silent shout-out to Source saying, 'Please help me to understand this aspect of myself, to love and set it free.' If you encourage all of your parts to step into the light, you will better assimilate them as you move into deeper transformation.

....

So, my suggestion for navigating difficult emotions up to this point is to remember your immensity, breathe and own what's coming up for you. The more you do this, the less sting your emotionality will have in its tail.

I don't mean to sound rude here, but **you might not completely understand what it's like to be a human in the grips of despair.** It takes more than remembering, breathing and accepting to make everything better!

My darling, I *do* understand, for I live vicariously through you! Need I remind you of all the snot-laden cries I have witnessed? Further, I have more recommendations to come.

So, let's say you are in the grips of despair. A gnarly emotion has clamped itself to your head like a deformed vulture. You have remembered your divine nature, breathed and acknowledged your emotions as yours. I next recommend that you *label* and *feel* them.

You can start by stating what you are feeling, something along the lines of, 'Right now, I am experiencing hatred, anger, grief, frustration, powerlessness, sadness, jealousy, anxiety, dread', (or whatever you happen to be feeling at the time). For argument's sake, let's imagine it's a sense of powerlessness. In this instance, you would say, 'Right now, I'm feeling powerless.' Then you would sit with that for a while.

Of course, you might prefer to indulge fantasies of pinching a perpetrator rather than immersing yourself in how you are feeling at this point, but you would be better served to truly *feel* what is going on for you at a deep level.

You rarely allow yourself to do this. Instead, you race to

understand the external source of your pain and be rid of the pain itself. '*They* did this to me. This happened *out there*. Now I will move as quickly as I can to cease feeling this way.' But allow me to let you in on a little secret: the earthly experience is a polarised one. You get to know happy and sad, safe and scared, anger and peace. You get to know both sides of the coin to reach the ultimate understanding that *happiness is what you are*. It is part of this crazy trip you chose to embark upon. It is through this journey that you transcend.

To experience this transcendence, I suggest that you sit solidly with your hatred, anger, grief, or whatever you're feeling, and ask, 'Where in my body am I feeling it? What shape is it? What colour? What sensation?' followed by the million-dollar questions:

What fear is driving this emotion?
What am I so afraid of?

Then, *bingo!* You are on course to revelation. It is imperative that you begin this enquiry before you run away with things like a gazelle with an arrow festooned to its butt; before your brain recklessly attributes false labels or blame to determine the quickest escape route to outsprint the pain.

You may first notice that your answers are based on suppositions that you are less than you are; that they are less than they are; that you are better than they are; that you are unlovable or broken; that you need to change; that somebody else needs to change to make you okay; that your painful feelings will never pass; that your situation will lead to complete devastation, desolation, destitution, incapacity, crippling loneliness, perpetual agony or inescapable hardship. But none of these things are necessarily true.

Redemption begins by saying things like, 'Despite this fear in the form of envy, I am more than okay. *I love myself*,' or 'Despite this rejection, I am amazing. *I love myself,*' or 'Despite this judgement, I am working on it. I am a great person and *I love myself,*' or 'Despite this anger, deep down I am scared and doing my best to understand why, and *I love myself anyway,*' or 'Despite feeling worthless, I am a jewel in the crown of the universe and *I love myself.* I encapsulate love. *I love, love, love myself!*'

It is about illuminating your 'injured' parts with self-love to facilitate healing. It is about loving yourself in the midst of your discomfort. It is about allowing love the freedom to move during your darkest hours and generating love even while you are in pain.

Remember, Love with a capital *L* trumps everything including emotions that aren't in alignment with what Source wills for you. It has the capacity to merge with how you are feeling to precipitate change. It can saturate and dissolve pain. It can help to remind you that the agony that is making you feel constricted, hurt, victimised, mistreated, stupid, unlovable, vulnerable, weak, furious, freakish, unattractive, grief-stricken, petrified or unwanted is in stark contrast to who you really are.

You're saying that I should feel my emotions, own them and love myself anyway. I like it! **I think one of the hardest parts will be to remember to practise this when I next have a meltdown!**

Don't worry. You will. I'll prompt you. But wait! There's more! And it is delicious!

After you have loved yourself, the next thing to do is *expand.*

When you experience that which you fear, your brain and body tend to contract. You recoil and shrink down. But let me tell you that *expanding* through difficult situations is incredibly empowering when it comes to reclaiming your balance.

Therefore, inhabit your body. Adjust your posture. Change your stance to that of a superhero. Stand tall, as though a helium balloon is attached to the top of your head, forcing you to lengthen your spine. Feel yourself rising to the challenge while regarding yourself as an indestructible warrior. Expand your awareness while examining things from a higher perspective.

By adopting the stance of Wonder Woman, you will be engaging your inner strength, tapping into your internal resources and sensing your power. By connecting with your core—where you are strong, safe and calm—growth will ensue.

Like I said, I just need to remember to do this when I next lose my sh**!

You will, my love. You will. That's why I'm here.

By now you have hopefully realised that you are far greater than your feelings. It is okay to experience them. The trick is not to get lost in them or over-identify with them, as you have done in the past. While your emotions may be like your children, they certainly aren't *you*!

Once you have engaged the above, you will be in a stronger position to call to mind how you would prefer to feel, for there does come a point where you do have a choice. You can choose to have steam billowing from your ears for the long haul, ruminating over your situation for years, or you can step back into your power and recognise that it's time to let go. You might even like to imagine your situation from an illuminated standpoint. If you were a fearless, enlightened being, how would you deal with this matter? How would your circumstances appear through your wise, brilliant eyes?

....

Although you do not yet believe me, it is possible to sit in a state of hell at the same time as being aware of the perfection of everything. Through the perfection part of the paradox, you will know true safety. If you are able to tap into this, you will know without doubt that an energy moves through you that has the capacity to transcend every fear.

Remember, you are a piece of God. You literally cannot be part of anything greater. You are *not* your pain. And although much of my instruction may seem simplistic, or even impossible, you will know you are getting somewhere when you start to choose how you respond to the human experience; when you realise you have different options available and pick those that are spiritually motivated.

We in the blobby stratosphere often joke that if Earth's human inhabitants paid as much attention to internal makeovers as they do external ones, the world would be a much better place! We want you to be well from the inside out. We want you to feel amazing. We want you to know that you are cherished and more than okay because you are what we are: light-filled, precious, vitally important and deserving of all good.

Regardless of how dire, despairing or dramatic things seem, you can always engage the energy we all share to generate greater compassion and forgiveness for yourself and others. Every single happenstance can be used to usher you closer to God. Again, you get to choose how you evolve in this lifetime, either kicking and screaming or forging ahead with dignity and grace.

A lot of your life revolves around the idea that you are damaged and in need of repair. You are not. Your inner turmoil is the result of you failing to shine love upon certain aspects of yourself. It is not from being wrong or wronged but from inadequately recognising your true self.

So, when you next find yourself consumed by life's problems, reach up, not down. Feel energy coursing through you. See your issues dwarfed against the magnitude of the ever-expanding universe. Breathe. Sit. Process. Grow. Request clarity, comprehension and composure. Be still and imagine a fresh, revitalising wave transmuting your unrest into peace. When you sit with your feelings and call upon the light, know in your heart of hearts that you are not only okay, but transforming from chrysalis to butterfly.

You have nothing to fear.

Exercise: How can you deal with difficult emotions?

No matter what you are experiencing, you are so much more than your feelings and circumstances allow you to see — *way* more. But it can be difficult to remember you are divine when consumed by spiky emotions such as anger or sadness. While in the throes of turbulence, a simple yet effective exercise is to say to yourself:

'Even in the midst of this storm, I love and appreciate myself.'

Or:

'Even in the midst of this storm, I am connected to All That Is and love myself.'

Or:

'Even though I'm quivering with rage and my eyes are about to explode, I am pure consciousness. I am love.'

By reciting these statements, or ones similar, you allow yourself a tiny reprieve to remember your true nature, which will allow you to shine love upon your troubling situation.

Remember, experiencing negative emotions isn't 'wrong'. It is okay to feel them and use them as a catalyst to experience your vastness.

You are immortal. You are indestructible. You are love.

Don't forget!

Cheat Sheet: Emotion

The moment you feel jagged emotions taking hold:

- *Remember* your immortality and immensity.
- *Observe* the parts of you that are steady and okay.
- *Breathe*, breathe. It won't be long now.
- *Accept* your emotions as you would your own children.
- *Feel* your emotions.
- *Ask* what fear lies behind them.
- *Love* yourself in the midst of your pain.
- *Expand* your physical body and spiritual awareness.
- *Engage* your inner strength and resources.
- *Process.*
- *Choose* how you would prefer to feel.
- *Heal.*
- While you may have created your emotions, they are not you.
- You are a gorgeous, melodious, vibrant and creative creature having a trippy experience within a generous, abundant, compassionate and altruistic universe.
- You were born to love.

Chapter 13. **Now**

Dear Blob,

Before I start blabbing, I would like to reiterate my gratitude to you for sharing your infinite wisdom. You've taught me so much, including that I am a little blob of consciousness in my own right. Yet I still scratch my head ... for unlike you, I have one to scratch. [*Ouch!*]

My question today concerns 'the now', which you casually threw into conversation somewhere along the line. I've read a bit about it. I've heard a lot about it. But I don't really get it.

What is 'the now'?
Why is it so important?
And do I really need to bother with it?

Kindest regards,
Spiritual Being Who Feels Closer to a Gorilla

Dear Great Gorilla,

At last you are beginning to wrap your head around the depths of your perfection. Comparing yourself to a gorilla is one of the greatest compliments you could ever pay yourself, for they are magnificent beasts, are they not, just as you are! And, like me, you are indeed a blob of consciousness. The fact that you referred to yourself like this proves that you are assimilating what we have discussed very well, so well, in fact, that I could almost cry. (I said 'almost', for being headless, I have no eyes through which to sprout tears, which is probably a good thing considering our work together will soon draw to a close.) [*Ouch!*]

....

But let us not detract from 'the now' for we are together in this moment and that is all we have. We need nothing else. We don't require anything more. If you keep thinking we do, you will keep waiting for something that never occurs ... because *this is it, now*.

You cannot *not* be in the now. You are the embodiment of God in this second, now. And in this one, and in this one. Hey, I could do this all day! But my point is:

This is it.
You are it.
Now is it.
And *now* is all there is.

Is that profound enough for you? Am I messing with your head? I hope not, because when you lock into the mindset that this is it, right now, and nothing needs to change, you will finally wake up, so let me illustrate this for you as clearly as I can.

The past has already happened. It exists only in your mind. The future is yet to come. It doesn't exist at all. So, if the past is beyond your control and the future isn't fixed, what are you left with?

Now?

Correct!

Your ego primarily exists by projecting itself into the past and future. So if the past is over and the future is yet to come, that means the ego's influence can be unplugged if you are fixed in the now. But I know how you roll, or, rather, how your ego rolls, and this is how the majority of your contemporaries' egos roll as well: the wistful part of you waits for a relationship to deliver what you seek, or new clothes, a better bank balance, career, car, home, body, government, country or state.

Whatever the desire, it exists beyond the moment and, as already discussed, the ego will never be satisfied no matter what you have. It will always place your so-called satisfaction somewhere in the distance. Once you get what you thought you wanted, it will move onto the next thing, forever dangling a carrot before you that remains slightly out of reach.

It is this relentless search for fulfilment that has you effectively saying '*not* now' when, in fact, what you seek already exists in the moment. Therein lies the secret. Therein lies your freedom. By detaching from your ego's projections, you will begin to experience the glory of now. And if you remain steadfast in wrapping your heart around each second, you will come to know a brand-new reality the likes of which you have never known before.

Yet the now is more than being mindful. It is living with expanded awareness from moment to moment. It is being consistently aware that you are moving *through* God and being moved *by* God. It is being conscious of consciousness itself. When you are able to perceive the uniqueness of each minute, you will find a gentle acceptance underpinning your every undertaking, and tell me with a straight face that *that* doesn't sound rad!

It does, Blob, it does! **And I really want to get this, but ... huh?** It's like my brain can't quite latch onto what you are saying.

Maybe your brain can't, but your spirit can. I concede that this is a difficult one, particularly when you live in a linear timeframe and are swimming through illusion, and especially if your life seems out of

....

whack and there are a thousand things demanding your attention. But even as you read this you can be aware of the now.

In this moment, you are okay. From a soul perspective, everything is perfect from one second to the next. Even when you are collecting the mail, your life is full of depth and significance. Weird, I know, but paradox is the language of the Universe, and all is as it should be.

I have already intuited what you are dying to say, so I will save you the time. Please don't be offended by my impression of you as I twirl my 'hair' and chew gum: 'I mean, who in their right mind would believe that all is as it should be when it comes to a twisted car wreck, a violent relationship, or living with Alzheimer's or through a pandemic?' to which I would respond, 'At a very deep level, your soul-needs are *always* being met.'

All circumstances arise to assist in your evolution, so whatever is occurring is not only powerful but essential. It may not always feel like it or make much sense, and things may seem random, but you are evolving by the minute according to a grand design. Meanwhile, your inner perfection never wavers, for it exists in the now.

So, keep doing what you're doing while recognising the now. Pay your roadside assistance, cough up your fines, catch your trains, right-click your mouse and observe your moods. Keep moving through life, your duties, relationships and the world with a keen awareness on the now. Observe it threading through all that you do, knowing that the right place to be is exactly where you are *now*.

If you are worried about how you will remain immersed in each second while dealing with life's demands, fret not. Each 'now' sets up the next. The more you relax into the wonder of this idea, the more you will remove anticipatory fear from what may come. You will ride a wave of positive momentum and notice that things have a tendency to work themselves out, as you have seen on countless occasions before.

....

Remember, you chose to incarnate for the challenge of flicking on the switch. Everything has been set up for a great illumination to take place, and the more you remind yourself that all is in order, the more you will see that nothing needs to change, for you are already full of explosive awareness in this very moment.

Further, you didn't join this rollercoaster ride ill-equipped. You are unbelievably resilient and resourceful. This is true of all people. There are those whose circumstances defy belief, yet they forge ahead from one second to the next. When you accept your life from moment to moment, as well as yourself, your fellows, your planet and the entire shebang that orbits it, the untold energy you've exerted in punching your way through life can be put to better use. It is up to you to draw on your strength and usher in the serenity that is found in the now, and I hope you will do this, for it's where your power lies.

To aid you in your quest, I again suggest that you call to mind who you are as often as you can. As a friendly reminder, you are immense, immortal, safe, precious and loved. You are love personified. In this second, you are connected to Source. Even if you were in a sludge-filled trench you would still be connected. No matter where you are or what you are doing, you are always connected, full stop, the end, right now, *kaboom*!

Feel the truth of this wash through your consciousness. Feel it override every fallacy you've ever dreamed up about yourself, including that you are a pathetic creature pandering to the whims of a world gone mad. Override all false ideas that pull you out of the moment. And do it *now*!

Oh, Blob. I really want to. But it's as though I can't quite take off. **Am I really ready for the now?**

....

Are you ever! But if you don't believe you are ready enough, good enough, pure enough or able enough to experience the now, then guess what? *You won't be.* If you want to inch closer to feeling it, keep dropping your lovely awareness into the stillness of your being throughout the day until you taste what I speak of. The now is there. The now is here!

Remember, there is an incredible, light-filled energy in and around you at all times that brims with pure, radiant love. The power, profusion and joy of this energy is found in the now. It is intoxicating and mind-blowing and yours for the taking.

The more you intend to experience it, the closer you will be, without the need for your circumstances to change. The now is primed to rush in and flood you with awareness, so yearn for it, call for it, and recall that it's here. Again, I remind you that you are powerful beyond your wildest imaginings, so keep asking for that gentle power to reveal itself in all its majesty and it will become evident.

Feel the inexplicable. Feel the divinity that is present *now.* Sense it. Keep your mind buoyed to the moment, and keep reminding yourself that perfection is right here, right now, all around, delicious and flawless. Don't try this once and forget about it. Do it till you experience it, till your cells tingle with excitement.

Are you beginning to understand this subject a little more? Your blank expression tells me that the answer is no! All I am suggesting is that you *be* from moment to moment — that you *experience* yourself 'being'. It's as 'simple' and mind-bending as that!

Just do your best to realise that all you have is now and that now is divine and sublime.

When you experience what I speak of, it will be all over, red rover.

The tug of war will end.

And you will be free.

Exercise: How can you experience the now?

To realise the now is to experience it *now*! There's no time like the present!

Begin by being still. Start to sense what it might be like to exist in the now and to feel the perfection of you, your spirit and your life—everything—in this very second. Stay with it until you start to feel something, perhaps a subtle shift that makes you feel empowered.

Now, get up and start moving through the world and introducing this feeling to what you do.

How does it feel to have an experiential understanding of the now? How does it feel to brush past another person and interact? What is it like to notice what your sight lands on? What is it like to be *you* in each moment? How does it feel to have the air kiss your skin? How does it feel for your body to move through divine consciousness? How does it feel to be aware from one second to the next? What's it like to feel charged by the potential of each moment? What's it like to be vigilantly, fiercely and wholeheartedly present as you relinquish thoughts of the future or past?

Dare I say *exhilarating*?

Dare I say *freeing*?

Try this as a short experiment before expanding the timeframe. Continue trialling it until you find yourself living it.

Your time starts … *now*!

Cheat Sheet: The Now

- *This* is it. Now. This second.
- There is nothing but this moment.
- You need nothing but this moment.
- What you seek already exists.
- Your life is exactly as it should be.
- The ego can only exist by projecting itself into the past or future.
- The ego can be unplugged if you focus on the now.
- The ego's relentless search for fulfilment is effectively saying '*not* now!'
- You are connected to Source in this second, now.
- Divinity is present in this second, now.
- Perfection is right here, right now.
- Even while taking care of business can you be aware of the now.
- Thread your expanded awareness through all that you do.
- *Be* from moment to moment.
- Feel the glory of now.
- Sense yourself moving through divine consciousness.
- You are moving through God.
- You are moved *by* God.
- You were born to love.

Chapter 14. *Meditation*

Dear Blob,

'Now' is probably the time to announce that I'm worried sick. You alluded last chapter that our time together may be drawing to a close. While I don't like to detract from the now, noooooo! Please don't go! I can't live without you! You have no idea how incredibly important you have become to me, or how much your guidance has meant.

But if you must go, can I ask another favour?

How do I bring everything we've discussed into play?

Is there a method I can use to drive it all home?

Please still be there!

I miss you already.

Namaste.

Dear Gentle Spirit,

Yep, still here. And, God, how much do I love you? Sure, I've got laser-trained ideas steadily focused on your brain from which you are intuiting your questions, but you always seem to ask just the right thing!

You've enquired about what you can do to bring everything into play, which I presume to mean an overarching tool that will facilitate all that we've discussed. And I do believe that the simple answer to that is *meditation* — pure and simple meditation ... definitely, absolutely, totally, without question. So, let us have a yarn about this, given that it just so happens to be another of my specialty subjects.

The importance of sitting in silence every day cannot be overstated, despite the modern world appearing specifically designed to distract you from anything remotely contemplative to keep you puffing and panting like a rat on a treadmill.

I would even go so far as to say that sitting in silence in your digital age has become so foreign that the prospect must seem as absurd as me suggesting you pop an iPhone into your mouth and attempt to digest it. And that would be just plain stupid, for how would you then be able to snap a photo of yourself eating a honey-drizzled waffle whilst in warrior pose wearing a bikini for the purpose of uploading it to Instagram?

Don't worry. You're not the only one who balks at the idea of meditation. And you can't really be blamed considering you've got a million other things to do, like groom, exercise, cook, clean, eat, drink, work, type, shop, commute, binge-watch and everything else in between. You don't have enough time, energy or patience. You're too tired. You just can't do it. *Dancing with the Stars* isn't going to watch itself. You've tried countless times to meditate at the end of your yoga class, only to fall asleep. And even if you *did* add it to your day's jam-packed agenda, your mind would undoubtedly pinball all over the place anyway.

There *is* all of that, but here's the God's honest truth: meditation creates a space that allows you just that — a *space* to bring into play all that we've talked about. *All of it!* And I'm not even kidding, which makes meditation *vitally* important, perhaps more than the things listed above.

Meditation will help you to know yourself, love yourself, love others, be more compassionate, be better able to problem-solve, connect, see through the illusion, understand why you're here, bypass the ego, drop judgement, think clearly, manifest, pray, manage your emotions, live in the now and step into the oneness of All That Is. Meditation is the gateway to enlightenment. It is the key to inner peace. I repeat:

Meditation is the gateway to enlightenment.
It is the key to inner peace.

Meditation will make you feel more centred, loving, powerful, resilient, placid, connected, protected, serene, wise, creative, balanced and wonderful. It doesn't get much better than that. It doesn't get much simpler. And it is possibly *the* most practical and easy-to-understand directive that I will ever bequeath you past remembering to take out the bin on Monday night!

Great! Where do I sign? **And how does it work?** Let's nail this bad boy!

Yes, let's!

It's difficult to articulate just how effective meditation is when in essence we're talking about sitting and waiting for 'nothing' to happen, and that 'nothing' just happens to be everything, so, rather than getting caught up in that little conundrum, let's start nice 'n' easy.

I urge you to sit quietly—for at least twenty-minutes out of your full sixteen waking hours (a mere 2 per cent of your day)— and accept whatever comes. That's it — a commitment to devote 2 per cent of your day ... to nothing! Okay, maybe there's slightly more to it than that, so let me proffer some further motivation.

You devote excessive time to recharging your phone, laptop and a myriad of other devices. It is paramount that you do likewise, from a spiritual point of view. The more charged up you are, the more resilient you will be. And similar to how your physical body can heal itself if the conditions are right, so too can your spiritual and emotional bodies be healed through meditation. By sitting quietly on a daily basis, you will begin to feel subtle movement in your own energy field, and as far as I'm concerned, that's a whole lot better than running yourself ragged and giving your power away.

Given your potency, cultivating your energetic prowess is not only beneficial to you but everyone around you, so I cannot emphasise the importance of sitting calmly and purifying your field enough. Through regular practice, that is what meditation achieves. It allows the true You to emerge in all its glory. Remember, the true You is immense and wonderfully aware, and meditation is an avenue to gain direct access to it.

You can meditate when you first wake up and/or before you go to sleep. It can be approached as though it's your own private laboratory in which you get to explore subtle energies and your connection to Source. Your lab can be entered at home or while sitting on a bus, train or plane.

By incorporating meditation into your daily routine, you will begin to feel something subtle building. Imagine exploring your inner world. Imagine the exhilaration of discovering your own glittering consciousness. Imagine the relief of bypassing your ego's barricades and realising that you are pure, loving and connected. Meditation can facilitate that and more!

Therefore, by making meditation a priority, you will be building upon all we've discussed. There is no need to approach it with dread. There is no need to break into a sweat. There is no need to tackle it as though it is the greatest challenge of all time, for that is the way of the ego. No, approach your practice softly. Allow yourself to be still. Allow yourself to nestle into your inner self where things are safe and warm. The more you do it, the more you will enjoy the fruits of your 'labour' because you will be building a bridge between the physical and metaphysical and plugging into the light.

When your do this regularly, you will more easily access your own equilibrium as you scuttle about doing your thing. Meditation will pool your resources and allow you to dip into them whenever you need to.

As I've mentioned many times now, the most desirable aspiration you can have is to experience your own sweet divinity. The more you exercise your will to connect with the Divine, the more your days will be ongoing experiential meditations through which you unify. You cannot focus on anything higher, purer or more perfect. This will open up to you more through meditation.

Remember, you are not stumbling through life like a sight-impaired aardvark, even though it might feel like it at times. Rather, you are guided by spirit more than you know. You are being continually propelled forward for the sake of your growth. Your spirit is always nudging you in the right direction, only its whispers often fall on deaf ears because you are so engrossed in Netflix. So how do you hear it? The answer, my friend, is through *meditation*, which allows you to be still enough to tune into the subtle energies that abound.

Point taken. And now for the million-dollar question:

How do I do it?

The purpose of our discussion today is not to provide you with a definitive 'how-to' guide, as there are already thousands of in-depth manuals and courses on how to meditate. However, to give you an idea of how to enter a meditative state, it is essentially a case of:

(a) getting comfortable,
(b) breathing,
(c) calming down,
(d) allowing the outer world to drop away,

....

(e) observing your chattering mind,

(f) detaching from your chattering mind,

(g) tuning into subtle energies,

(h) expanding, and

(i) blissing out.

When you pause to meditate, some suggest that you inhale deeply and breathe in the light. I personally like this recommendation, as it means you are receiving living energy and allowing it to permeate your mind, body and soul.

At the start of meditation, you may notice your thoughts leapfrogging through your mind. Note how they jump from one thing to the next — directionless, erratic, incessant. Catch the subject matter and remember that the narrative you're listening to is literally designing (and possibly ruining) your life! Let's not forget that your thoughts shape your reality.

Nothing more will compel you to drop the psychotic drivel than noticing your thoughts during the initial stages of meditation. Rather than being concussed by their pettiness, you will hopefully be moved to push beyond the unease that they cause. The trick is to observe them with detachment. Don't judge. Just notice. Sense the greater You taking charge and allow yourself to coast upon the ensuing stillness. Your crazy thoughts may continue, but you will have risen above them.

To help reach this point, gently affirm that you wish to experience stillness *now*. Mean it, and your awareness will be airlifted beyond everyday thought, and there you will bask. Here things are still. You will know you have arrived when you no longer indulge the internal dialogue that includes things like, 'I am not good enough,' 'I've got to do this,' 'I've got to do that,' 'He did this,' 'She did that,' 'Work sucks,' 'I'm out of milk,' 'My neck's ugly,' 'What's that? A *fly*?'

When you begin to engage the bigger You, your attention will

....

be drawn from the chatter of your everyday mind to something deeper, bigger, vaster, richer and far more profound. You will find yourself in concert with a pulsing, powerful yet delicate force that is so immense that you may sigh.

As this intensifies, you may even go down to the molecular level to direct every piece of you to let go of any ego-based thoughts, feelings, beliefs and tensions that no longer serve you. While the little you may wrestle and writhe, the bigger You will have little trouble in setting such things free.

Express your desire for optimal silence and thy will be done. Assert that the time to be calm is *now*. When you experience the stillness, there is nothing you will want more than to quieten your mind and feel that quality of peace. And as you meditate regularly, your energy will build given meditation's cumulative effect.

That sounds brilliant, Blob. **Are there any other benefits to meditation** to help psyche me up?

There are so many, my love, that I don't know where to start!

Going within and enjoying that space is a thousand times more reliable than paying attention to the external world, which tosses and turns relentlessly. I remind you again that what you focus on becomes real, so unless you check in with the stillness, you will be constantly pulled into the riptides of the ego-world with little input into the direction you head. You will remain trapped in the mindset of being an aging, physical unit on the fast train to death, forever ignorant of your enduring perfection.

Meditation creates a reprieve from such fallacies. It is nutritious for the soul. It is a tool to pull you back from life's dramas and remember your truth. Through this simple, precious ritual, you can stay topped up on Source energy and satiate your soul.

Like I have said before, there is a part of you that already knows how to do this stuff. It knows how to enter a state of meditation, so it's not a case of technique as much as it is you exerting a desire to get there. Use your consciousness as your guide and drift to a place that surpasses lower thought; where baseness is replaced by lightness; where noise is replaced by silence; where you vibrate with love and recall who you are from your own sacred space.

If I may remind you of who you are at this juncture, you are an incredible divine entity pulsating with perpetual, enduring, white-hot love, full of compassion, ecstasy and peace. As you go deeper into meditation, you will see these qualities more for yourself. You will feel your spirit lifting and your mind flooding with tranquillity. You will see that you embody pure, uncorrupted, unconditional, unadulterated, take-your-breath-away Love with a capital *L*.

Again, I urge you to drop the two-dimensional idea of love. Think bigger, vaster, grander, incorruptible love and you are getting warmer. It is *in* you. It *is* you. You are it. It is potent, glorious, precious and powerful. It is always available. To submerge into its depths is to relinquish your fears, and you are in a position to surrender to this every day through the medium we are discussing.

And guess what? Every contemplative second draws you closer to the centre of your being where truth prevails, where your completeness awaits and where consciousness dwells in its purest form.

So, meditation is your vehicle to traverse deep within and discover the Holy Grail of your own magnificence and tenderly reveal the contentment of your soul, for you will be reuniting with the real You, which is so resplendent, that it's enough to make even Gandalf blush!

....

What should I expect?

That is difficult to answer because meditation is subjective, and each experience is different. However, you may become conscious of that which hosts you, as in your flesh-and-bone home. You may begin to feel the 'largeness' of your spirit filling the room. You may no longer feel your hands. You may simply enjoy the peace of pausing for a while. You may feel as though you are entering a void filled with energy. You may see lights cruising behind your eyelids. You may sense that you are divinity existing within divinity. Occasionally, you may even feel slightly uncomfortable, if not challenged, by your everyday thoughts, in which case it is advisable to breathe and embrace whatever presents itself with curious detachment.

Many different experiences can be had through meditation, too many to mention. One of the most special, however, is sensing an immensely loving energy that is so vast and benevolent that you will feel held and at peace. This can be viewed as the emergence of the real You, higher self or Source, whichever you choose, for they are all part of the One.

Once you get into the habit of sinking into the depths of your being, life will become meditation in motion, where peace moves with you as you move through the world with purity leading the way. Everything will take on a richer hue. Your day-to-day life will become easier to manage. You will drop into your heart centre more easily and exist from a place of equanimity, balance and beauty. You will be better shielded from the world's temperamental ego constructs. Your urge to indulge banal thoughts will decrease. Traffic jams will less likely do your head in!

Meditative states can also assist when you need to make big

decisions by turning things over to your inner guide and asking how to proceed. In time, you will learn to differentiate between your ego's voice and that of your higher self. You will begin to regard your lower thoughts as clouds and your elevated ones as the unchangeable blue sky that exists perennially in the background — poised, calm, immense and forever overseeing what is best for you and your grand development.

But, hey, I can explain all of this till the cows come home. You've heard it all before. Reading about it is wonderful in terms of gleaning information, but I can assure you that *experiencing* meditation is something else entirely. You just need to make the time, the choice and commitment, and decide that you want to experience it for yourself. Ask for help, intend and *do*. Then you will!

Before signing off, I'd like to make a sweeping statement here, so please humour me for just a moment. Until you practise meditation, you will likely never feel quite right. Until you finally come to understand that you and Source are deeply entwined, you will feel misaligned and off balance. Meditation can restore that equilibrium and usher in the revelation that you are connected. You are safe, always have been and always will be. You have nothing to fear.

When you really begin to understand this, I am sure you will reverently reach for meditation to embody more of what I speak of. Within the stillness, your brain's incessant diatribe will be silenced. Your thoughts will naturally align, and so too will your words and actions. You will more effortlessly love yourself, others, Source and your life. You will experience a richer, peace-filled incarnation and see through the illusion. Your emotions will be more balanced and your mind better disciplined. You will forgive more readily, be in the moment and be closer to enlightenment.

Now, tell me without your nose growing that that doesn't sound amaze-balls! Om shanti, Dear One. Om shanti to the max!

....

Exercise: How can you meditate?

There are literally thousands of meditation techniques, but the art is less about technique and more about experience. Let us focus on the *experience* you derive from this simple exercise, which can be used as a catalyst to investigating meditation further.

Begin by getting comfortable in a seated position, closing your eyes and drawing deep breaths into the depths of your lungs. Allow yourself to drift away from your chattering mind. Drop down to where it feels safe, be it within your heart or deep down inside. Use each breath to draw you further into your being, where truth and serenity reside. Begin to notice your genuine identity coming more to the fore as you explore consciousness in its purest form.

Be aware of *life* pulsing through you. Sense a luminous ball of light inside you. Notice its colour. Merge with it. Imagine brilliant white luminosity extending from you, outward, upward, forward and backward, into the future and past, infusing 'the now', emanating powerfully yet blissfully from the Source within you, infusing all in its path.

Connect with any positive feelings that arise. Take them with you into your daily life and call them to mind as frequently as you can, be it ten times a day or a hundred. Sense the love, peace, wisdom, compassion, patience, lightness and joy as you go about your business, until you *are* love, peace, wisdom, compassion, patience, lightness and joy.

The aim of meditation is to sink deliciously into the depths of your being and gain a sense of security and clarity as you reunite with Source. Indulge it. Get cosy with it. Recalibrate. Enjoy love's company and know without doubt that it is in you.

Cheat Sheet: Meditation

- Meditation will help you to know yourself, love yourself, love others, be more compassionate, problem-solve, connect, see through the illusion, understand why you're here, bypass the ego, drop judgement, think clearly, think highly, manage your emotions, live in 'the now' and step into oneness.
- Meditation makes you more centred, loving, patient, powerful, resilient, placid, connected, protected, serene, wise, creative and wonderful.
- It is the gateway to enlightenment.
- It is the key to inner peace.
- Meditation creates a space away from the world's drama and illusion.
- Meditation is nutritious for the soul.
- It is the way within.
- It helps restore equilibrium.
- Meditation helps you gain access to the real You.
- Meditation helps you to love yourself, others, Source and life.
- It helps you to travel more peacefully.
- It helps to build a bridge between the physical and metaphysical.
- Meditation quietens banal, everyday thoughts.
- Meditation involves getting comfortable, stilling, breathing, calming, detaching, observing, tuning into subtle energies, expanding and blissing out.
- It is a spiritual recharge.
- It is a doorway to love.
- And you were born to love!

Chapter 15. *Death*

Dear Blob,

Om shanti right back at ya! What can I say? You make meditation sound hugely appealing, so I will definitely be practising my little head off to see how I go.

In the meantime, you've mentioned on countless occasions that I'm immortal. You've also referred to the 'fast train to death', which piqued my interest and raised the big question:

What happens when I die?

Being an old goth at heart, I'm 'dying' to hear what you have to say!

Cordially yours,

Wannabe-Mrs-Robert-Smith

Dear Granny Smith,

I am glad you've been paying attention. I have indeed intimated on several occasions that there is no such thing as 'death', for when you 'die', the real You continues to thrive. When you die, you return to your natural, spiritual form, a phenomenal transition though which you become wholly aware of your true self, if you didn't manage to accomplish this while you were 'alive'.

Confused? Don't be. Just know that when you die, it is only your physical body that perishes, and I pray that this provides you with some consolation rather than fear.

Considering you noted my immortality references, you probably also grasped my inference that you are distinct from your body, which I shall extrapolate upon now. When you die, you will feel little attachment to the gorilla suit from which you recently departed!

....

I mean that with no disrespect. You will of course recognise that your body served you, but feel no great loss over its denouement despite the vast amounts of attention you paid to its appearance, maintenance and upkeep when you were alive.

You may even begin to wonder why you identified so heavily with it in the first place and conclude that you were a lot less hot than you thought! I do not say this to discourage you from taking good care of yourself, but in the hope that you will once and for all wrap your head around the fact that *you are not your body.*

I jest in relation to your hotness levels, by the way. You are totally hot! But I am making the point that when you die, you will see your body as little more than a versatile sack of anatomy that manoeuvred you through the world as you lived your amazing life. As I said in one of our earlier discussions, your body is closer to an avatar driven by your spirit ... and ego.

However, you asked what happens when you die, so I'll stop jabbering about your hot bod and unveil what is perhaps life's greatest mystery.

The death experience is like coming to life after lying dormant for a thousand years. It is a literal return to consciousness, free of physical restraints. It is a grand awakening, a resurrection of sorts.

Upon 'death', you will be drawn to the light like a moth to the flame. Your perception will expand and your metaphysical eyes will open to the splendour of reality. Rather than inhabiting your body, you will inhabit *awareness* and wake up to all that I've described during our chats, including the fact that you are a divine, dazzling, unlimited, immense, serene, peaceful and powerful entity exploding with love!

Your every question will be answered: *who* you are, *what* you are, *why* you are, and each revelation will come as a staggering burst of remembrance that is nothing short of euphoric.

You will be struck by the powerful realisation that you really *are* immortal and indestructible. You will know without doubt that you never end; that nobody does. And you will see that you are destined to exist as an energetic being for all of eternity.

Whoa! Okay, keep going. **This is trippy! Where will I go?**

Words don't do it justice, but let's give it a try.

The space that you will immediately occupy is a realm of peace beyond your wildest conception. You will know this place. You will remember it. You will sense that you have been here before. You will feel wholly welcomed, accepted, expected, embraced and *loved*. Oh, how loved you will feel! So pure is this love, so beyond your earthly experience, that you will be overcome by ecstasy. You will feel exquisitely free and a million times more enlivened than you did while you were in the body. You will sense that you have *arrived*. You know that you *belong*.

Your arrival will be imbued with a deep sense of oneness that will quench any loneliness, separateness or alienation you experienced on Earth. Acceptance, rapture and serenity will be yours. Joy, harmony and bliss will prevail — states that you forgot were possible owing to the chaos of the world.

Never will you have felt so safe and protected. You will know with 100 per cent certainty that you chose to incarnate to surpass all obstacles to love. You will see that your life was not only courageous, but important, and this 'knowing' will come by way of epiphanies that will explode one after the other.

There will be no time, no future, no past. You will be immersed in the now and simply be, which is why accomplishing this while in physical form is such an incredible achievement that shows just how brave, skilled, resilient, determined, multifaceted and highly evolved you are regardless of the form you took and restrictions it imposed.

If you didn't manage to do so while you were alive, you will see through the illusion of your earthly experience with absolute clarity. You will see that you were always considered precious and cocooned by the light. Your spiritual amnesia, human frailty, challenges and anxieties will lift, and you will be Home.

Your ego will be no more, meaning the fear you once felt will be obsolete, and a joyous homecoming will be thrown in your name. Light energies will surround you in a hero's welcome. You will be celebrated like no other. You will feel adored and cradled. You will be asked things like, 'How did you go?' and, 'Did you manage to love and serve despite all the curveballs?'

You will notice everything pulsing with love. *Everything!* You may even see me exploding with pride in the background before thundering toward you and smothering you in my most heartfelt embrace! And the hugs won't end there. You will be enveloped by the All.

You will be in a euphoric space marvelling over the glory of love and the unparalleled freedom devoid of physical restriction. Your movements will be fluid and graceful. You will communicate by way of thought. Your perception will intensify. You will see explosive colour never before seen and hear glorious melodies never before heard.

Your post-death experience will be an outright revelation that feels more 'real' than any reality you knew on Earth. Your human life will begin to take on the qualities of a fast-fading dream, which is why I quoted from the rhyme *Row, Row, Row Your Boat* so long ago. Your current life *is* but a dream, and coming to this realisation will be epiphanic indeed.

Oh, dear Blob. This makes me want to cry! Will I deserve this?

Won't I be judged?

Ah, the ol' judgement thing. It comes up every time! Let me get comfortable so that I can explain this as best I can.

After you die, you will see that most of your materialistic, monetary and reputational endeavours were meaningless unless they were motivated by love. You will see that each unloving act perpetrated by you contravened Universal Law. Your just-lived life will roll out before you, scene by scene, as will the repercussions of your actions. You will vividly see, feel and experience what you did to other beings *from the perspective of those other beings*. In other words, every hurt you ever inflicted will be felt by you as *your* pain. I would like you to reread those sentences to comprehend the gravity of their meaning, for it lends much food for thought.

I am saying that you will jump inside another's skin and experience firsthand how your actions made that person feel, such as belittled, wounded, betrayed, humiliated, unloved, misunderstood, wretched or broken. You will literally suffer the anguish you seared onto others' hearts through your poor behaviour. Similarly, you will experience the joy you bestowed through your commendable actions, particularly those that involved love, compassion, service and positive contribution. You will see the ripple effect of both your positive and negative actions and how they impacted all things.

When you understand that you inflicted pain as a result of your own suffering, you will experience self-compassion. You will be surprised by the degree to which your unkindness was motivated by fear. Although your human life matters more than you know, the difficulties you endured were but a tiny blip within infinite eternity. But it will be clear that within that tiny timeframe, your life was full of purpose.

....

In relation to being judged, contrary to popular belief, the only spiritual being meting out 'punishment' on the other side will be your own sweet self by way of your regret and disappointment over not always loving to the best of your ability. There will be no judgement aside from your own. No ethereal force is going to give you a smack, demand you atone or condemn you to eternal suffering. Rather, you will see that you were enduringly loved and supported throughout your incarnation and afforded compassion even during your times of transgression. That support only continues.

Trust me, experiencing others' pain through your actions has a profound effect and is far more impactful than being on the receiving end of a deity's disdain. You will wish that you had done a lot better than you did and feel incredible empathy for those that you hurt. Thanks to your newfound insight, you will crave others' forgiveness and forgive yourself for who you thought yourself to be. Likewise, you will forgive others.

It will be exceedingly apparent that your life played out just as it needed to for the sake of everyone's evolution, and that its synchronistic design could not have been more precise. Even if you did not learn every lesson, the people and situations you found yourself in were exactly what were needed to love, serve and grow. Your spirit was beyond efficient in having you experience all that you did.

Yes, my lovely, you are destined to realise that everything played out in accordance with your soul-driven motivations. You will see how interconnected everything is and that there were never any mistakes other than those that contravened love.

I'm just trying to understand, then, the point of trying to live a spiritual life on Earth. If I'm loved and forgiven for my transgressions and return to my perfect self when I die, then **why should I strive to master what we've been discussing while alive?**

Ah! I anticipated this question, so allow me to refer to a list of commitments you made before you were born. You set yourself the challenge of:

- *Remembering your true nature despite the trials of living on Earth.*
- *Shining light into the world so that others might see.*
- *Helping to bring an end to the fallacy of separation.*
- *Awakening from the dream despite being spellbound by illusion.*
- *Learning to love during times of adversity.*

Why were you crazy enough to attempt such an undertaking, I hear you ask?

Because you are a spiritual warrior determined to excel!

As I said many pages ago, you incarnated into human form to get amongst it, to experience the strangeness of being a seemingly separate entity negotiating a virtual non-reality while attempting to shake off spiritual amnesia. It's a highly skilled game you're playing, and you entered it by choice because you really, *really* wanted to master it at a deep level.

You volunteered to hold out a tiny torch to assist those who

....

are lost; to those who worship their egos, power, control, materialism, fear, separation and terror with little thought for much else; and to relinquish these things in yourself.

You hoped to play a role in bringing everyone Home with less regret in their hearts, knowing that every contribution you make adds to human evolution and raises the consciousness of the whole.

If that isn't enough to highlight the significance of your life, then I don't know what is!

Darling, you were born with a sliver of insight that allows you to sense that feeling separate from Source isn't worth the pain that it causes. There is a part of you that knows that divine connection is worth striving for. You sense that your world isn't quite right, and that 'not-quite-rightness' boils down to the multifaceted madness that abounds compounded by spiritual amnesia to which most have submitted.

So, while you're on Earth, you don't seek to reconnect with your spiritual self and Source for the sake of gaining favour or avoiding damnation. You do not avoid 'sin' for the purpose of reward. Rather, you strive to shorten the distance between you and God. Why? Because it feels wonderful, natural and more in alignment with how things ought to be. You strive to connect while moving through planetary density because it is the one truth that shines behind the illusion.

You strive to reconnect with Source because it hurts not to.

By now, you are coming to understand the extent of your divine nature and the fact that you are, and always will be, connected to God. That understanding will be made even clearer when you 'pass away'. When that time comes, you will see that you are, and always were, an extension of Source consciousness; that you are, and always were, never separate from it; that you are, and always were, a point of light amid countless light forms. You will appreciate that the trick of illusion helped to contrast the difference between connection and separation, and that in some ways it was a gift to help set you free.

If you don't come to this realisation during your lifetime, you will definitely see it post-death, understanding that what I've said is true: love, perfection, harmlessness and fearlessness are inherent in you. You are an incredible entity glimmering with blinding love. Your spirit is impeccable. You are pure divine consciousness. You are immortal. You are perfect. Your essence is dazzling. Source energy, ecstasy and peace dwell at your core.

When all is said and done, there is a very strong chance that you will shriek, 'Good God! Blob was right!'

Ha, ha! I do hope that's true! What you've been sharing is fascinating. **Is there anything else you'd like to impart about dying while I do my best to live?**

Yes! Let's start with a recap.

You will experience the real You through death, which is what I've been urging you to practise throughout our conversation. You will experience the magnificence of your soul. You will know with absolute certainty that you were always a spiritual being having a human experience. You will recognise that the Universe is conscious. You will communicate with a host of loving entities with no need for words.

Curiosity, awe and wonder will fill you. Universal knowledge will dawn on you with crystal clear clarity. You will have unrestricted access to cosmic wisdom, and a deep remembrance and understanding of everything you've ever wanted to know. You will vibrate with that knowledge and easily comprehend the profound information being downloaded to you, which I have done my best to distil throughout our discourse. You will absorb everything as though you are a sponge!

As you meld further with the Universe, your perception will sharpen. You will see that you were never alone. You will come to appreciate how deeply important your Earth mission was and how every occurrence played out according to a well laid-out plan, which slotted perfectly into the fabric of the cosmos. Your purpose was to love and serve. You will *know* this with blinding lucidity. And you will be proud of the countless achievements you made while in human form.

At the end of the day, beautiful friend, you are destined to be reabsorbed by the light. An intimate merging awaits that would steal your breath away if you had the need for air. Eternal love is fated to wash through you of an intensity that a human being could barely withstand.

And here is the big one:

When this happens, you will vibrate with the unshakable knowledge that *only love is real.*

That's the whole point!

It's the whole point of *life*!

Exercise: How can you feel more alive?

While in bed tonight, imagine your spirit filling the room. If you find yourself bogged down by ideas of limitation—dwelling upon insufficiencies, which are nothing more than earthbound suppositions—expand beyond them.

A sense of lack keeps you feeling small and tethered to fear and your limited self. This is far removed from who you really are, so expand your way through anything that makes you feel 'less than'. Focus on your immortal spirit with all that you have.

Visualise a cleansing, healing force emanating from the depths of your loving self. See that energy in your mind's eye rising upward and outward, enveloping your mind and body, infusing you with perfection.

Instruct yourself that it is time to let go of any habitual patterns that impede your awakening.

Whisper to every fibre of your being that transformation is underway.

Experience your *true self* in compliance with the challenge you set before you were born.

Cheat Sheet: Death

- Dying is akin to awakening from a deep coma.
- Dying is a return to consciousness after bursting free of physical restraint.
- Post-death, your just-lived life will take on the qualities of a fast-fading dream.
- You will see through the illusion.
- You will become acutely aware of your spiritual self.
- You will realise that you were never your body.
- You will see that you were a spiritual being having a human experience.
- You will have unrestricted access to universal knowledge.
- Your every question will be answered.
- Your awareness will expand.
- You will feel content, embraced, adored, cradled, complete, safe, protected, loved, accepted, connected, rapturous and serene.
- You will review your just-lived life.
- You will see the futility of your materialistic, monetary and reputational endeavours.
- You will see the ripple effect of your actions.
- You will be disappointed by your failings.
- You will understand that you are connected to Source.
- You will see that you were never alone.
- You will see that love, perfection, harmlessness and fearlessness were ever present.
- You will see clearly that your purpose was to love and serve.
- You will know that you are immortal and indestructible.
- You will know that only love is real.
- You will know unequivocally that you were born to love!

....

Chapter 16.
Enlightenment

Dear Blob,

Okay, as you can see, your last chapter resonated so deeply with me that I'm having a bit of a moment. Your description of death was, well, ... beautiful!

I am incredibly grateful to you for everything you have taught me. Because of you, I have appreciated who I am more. I have felt my awareness increase. I have observed my ego. I have exercised greater love. I have prayed. I have beckoned Source. I have improved my way of thinking. I have created. I have expanded. I have sat with my emotions. I have become more conscious of the now. My meditations have deepened. My understanding has heightened, and my circumstances have improved out of sight.

You have literally changed my life!

So please don't let this be over. I'd happily chat with you till the day I die ... and beyond.

Having said that, **I haven't reached a state of enlightenment yet**, so your work here is hardly done, which means you can't possibly go anywhere.

I'm crossing everything, including my eyes, in the hope that you will remain and continue our conversation.

I love you, Blob ... with all of my heart.

With utmost respect,

Your Humble Human Apprentice

xxx

Dear Wondrous Spirit,

You possess all the sweetness of a child, and I love you dearly too. But I am sure you know as well as I do that your progress hasn't been solely down to me. It has been down to your *remembrance*. And I will never leave you because 'you' and 'I' are one, so listen out for my whispers for I will always be near.

Rest assured that we can formally pick this up again in the future, but for now, I'd like you to bundle what we've discussed so far into a little package and share it with whomever cares to listen: those who possess the same burning curiosity as you; the seekers of knowledge; the finders of truth; those who have a niggling sense that there is more to life than meets the eye; those who sense that *they* are more; those who burn to at last see; those who burn to live these words; those who desire to walk the talk. There are millions craving remembrance, so do your best to disseminate what we've covered during this very important time of awakening.

Now, give me a second to switch off the booming reverb effect I added to my voice and hop off this cloud. It's time to get chatty again!

Okay, so what was it you asked? Oh, that's right. Nothing. So, allow me to formulate a question on your behalf:

Dear Blob, How do I step into a state of enlightenment and stay there so that the revelations you've described will actually be experienced during my wonderful incarnation?

That's what you wanted to ask, yeah?

Well, yeah. I couldn't have put it better myself!

But of course! Don't you know who I Am?

So ... we have finally arrived at the point of enlightenment. Like we weren't there already.

First, congratulations on choosing to drop the heavy armour of your ego and embrace the magnitude of your true self, for that is what enlightenment is all about. Second, the 'methodology' of stepping into the light and remaining there is so simple that it's difficult for me not to crease up!

I don't mean to sound flip, but to be enlightened is to *live everything I've been banging on about, chapter after chapter.* Remember who you are. Remember that your thoughts create your 'reality'. Remember the connection between you and your people and all other sentient beings. Remember your connection to the Divine. Remember to love, serve and observe. Remember not to over-identify with the bizarre machinations of your ego. Remember not to get caught up in the turmoil of the outer world. Remember the now. Remember to meditate and pray, and that you and Source are one.

Enlightenment means putting all this together and *doing* it, so let's drive this bad boy home. It's time to call on higher powers to assist you in experiencing it. Lock into the power of thought. Recognise the light blazing inside you. Be aware of your awareness. Feel it growing in strength and power. Feel it filling the spaces inside and beyond you, expanding farther and farther into the ether. *Feel* yourself enlightened.

Glorious friend, nothing I've suggested is out of your reach. *Nothing!* Nor should anything I've mentioned be considered a one-off folly. It is impossible to integrate everything we've discussed by turning to the last page, folding your arms and saying, 'Done! From now on, I shall manifest a magical life like a wizard on steroids and begin walking on water!' It is equally impossible to integrate all we've discussed through prising your eyelids open with matchsticks and rereading our musings for the thousandth time.

No, this piece of work is offered in its entirety as a design for life. I therefore urge you to *practise* all that I've said until an enlightened way of being comes naturally to you. Continually pull your awareness away from the world's distractions and place it within, forever reminding yourself of your inherent perfection and connection to the All. Keep reminding yourself that you are a radiant being of light and that all is as it should be.

Build the love within you, layer upon layer, as you move through your exquisite life. Devotedly incorporate meditation, invocation and reminders of your divinity into your routine. Be clear that living lovingly, spiritually and in an enlightened way is precisely what you intended before you were born. Surrender, then *do it*!

But what is enlightenment?
Can you explain what you mean?

To be enlightened is to see beyond the illusion. It is to wake up from the dream. It is to think clearly, see the world for what it is and truly grasp that you are an illuminated being; that you are a piece of Source having a curious human experience. It is to live with that understanding and a whole lotta love burning in your heart.

As I have repeatedly said, Source is *so* much more than an idea. It is a benevolent, jaw-dropping explosion of energy. It is vast, eternal and devastatingly powerful. I again fear that I am falling short because words cannot adequately convey what I am attempting to describe. But, as I've reiterated over and over again, *you* are part of *that*. *You* are a benevolent, jaw-dropping explosion of love — vast, eternal and incredibly powerful. You are *dazzling*. Do you hear me? Do you understand me? Do you believe me? *You are that.* You are made of the same stuff as God, meaning you already possess all the necessary ingredients to live as an enlightened being.

The supreme force that some refer to as God is not separate from you. It is not 'out there' in a galaxy far, far away. It isn't a being

....

perched on your shoulder whispering that it's wrong to spit on the footpath. The supreme force that some refer to as God is here, now, within you, within every person, within everything, including every molecule, particle, atom and cell. You and God are one, as are all people. Give yourself permission to drop all ideas of separation that suggest otherwise. Allow yourself to *experience* what I'm saying. If you can truly grasp this and allow it to fill you with wonder, your mind will be blown free of illusion.

There is as much Source energy now, in this moment, as there will ever be. You don't have to wait for a particular date in the distant future when the stars are perfectly aligned for your soul to be cleansed. Source is ever-present in its purest form, here, now, and it will never go away. It is in everything *now* — in, of and around you. By even daring to dwell on this idea and others like it, you are raising your power and positively charging the field around you. By embodying this idea, and others like it, you are igniting the world.

I so want to grasp this. **But ... I ... can't!**

Yes, you can! I know I have shared difficult concepts with you throughout this discourse. I know you're thinking, 'How can a creature with nasal hair possibly compare itself to God?' But believe me, you can! Do your best to experience the enormity of my words with your inner knowing rather than the synapses of your brain. Just try. Then don't try at all. Allow the bounty within to gently reveal itself and things will never be the same again.

Through meditation and the plethora of other techniques we've discussed, you can sink into a blissful state of peaceful recognition, where you can rest easy in the knowledge that everything is as it should be and carry that into your days. You are okay. You are safe.

You always have been and always will be. Source energy is with you. Benevolence. Love. Vastness. Power. Brilliance. Immortality. Purity. Awareness. These are all alive in you. Embracing this fact will lead you to liberty. So, strive to tap into it and continue doing so. There is magic in every second. *Feel* it and you will come to know life in a way that transcends everything that you have ever known.

I think you already get that you can't rely on your ego to help you to awaken. It will only keep telling you that my words are woo-woo and you must look outside yourself to find what you seek. But I pray that you will come to realise that there is nothing external to you that will deliver what you want, and that includes enlightenment. Nothing external will produce the inner peace that you crave.

However, I want you to know without reservation that actualisation is an absolute possibility for you in this lifetime. By consistently imagining what it might feel like to be enlightened, you draw it closer. Imagine the exhilaration as you dynamically glide through each second, and you will reel it closer.

If you would like to know why you are not yet enlightened, why you live in hope of transforming as your face gradually sags, it is because you don't allow yourself to see that you *already are*, that you are *already it*. It is because you focus so steadily on fleeting things in this mini creation of yours that you haven't yet experienced the enduring transcendence that enlightenment brings.

I am saying that your greatest barrier to enlightenment is the belief that you are not already enlightened!

Enlightenment is already here.

The illumination you seek is already within.

You need look no further to discover more divinity than exists in this moment. You can experience enlightenment now, in this second, for serious! So, tune into your sweet divine self and there it will be. Ta-da!

The purpose of our dialogue has been to remind you of your spiritual majesty. You chose this incarnation to love, serve and grow, to explore your own inner world and share your findings with the world in an explosion of light that helps reignite the planet. You chose this incarnation to wake up from the dream.

With my deepest respect, I commend you, beautiful human, for having the guts to explore with an open heart and mind, for holding up a tiny torch in a 'world gone mad', for taking the time to listen and put into practice all that I've said.

It has been my absolute honour to serve you and for us to share this special time.

I love you more than you will ever know, which is to say I love myself ... because we are one!

You are a beacon of light.

You are alchemy in motion.

Now go forth and prosper.

Live what we have discussed.

You are more than close.

You are already there.

I adore you with all of my being.

Eternally yours,

Blob ;) <3 xx

Exercise: How can you experience enlightenment?

Turn your awareness inward, toward any blocks that prevent you from experiencing enlightenment. You may be surprised to discover that within your personal rulebook there are reams of small print that rival even the most complicated of insurance policies, full of disclaimers and exceptions.

'I'll experience enlightenment once I stop being a judgemental maniac,' or 'I'll experience enlightenment once I learn to love the person who steals my sandwiches from the lunchroom,' or '... when I swear less,' or '... when I quit drinking,' or '... when I stop losing my temper,' or '... when the Illuminati loosens its grip on globalisation!'

Examine the conditions you place on experiencing spiritual awakening. When you begin to notice the barriers you place between 'you' and 'it', you will begin to appreciate them for what they are: spectres! Watch them evaporate as you recognise their vapidness, for nothing can really stand in the way of your connection to Source. Nothing! You are connected and switched on right here, right now, and always will be, regardless of whether you believe you're deserving enough, good enough or shiny enough.

Now, pass me my sunglasses, for your luminosity is blinding!

Cheat Sheet: Enlightenment

- *Live* the contents of this book.
- *Feel* yourself enlightened.
- Be *aware* of your awareness.
- Remember your connection to all beings.
- Remember your connection to the Divine.
- Remember that your thoughts are pivotal to your enlightenment.
- Remember to love.
- Walk the talk.
- Pull your awareness from the world's distractions and place it within.
- The illumination you seek is inside you.
- Move beyond logic.
- Drop the ego's heavy armour.
- Source is here, now, in every cell, molecule and atom.
- Source is a benevolent, jaw-dropping explosion of love — vast, powerful, dazzling and eternal, as are you.
- You and Source are one. Grasp this truth, and your mind will be blown free of illusion.
- You already possess all the necessary ingredients to be enlightened.
- You are already *there*. You are already *it*.
- You are a radiant being.
- All is as it should be.
- Be grateful every day for the gift of living a human life.
- You are okay. You are safe. You always have been and always will be.
- Your greatest barrier to enlightenment is believing that you are not already enlightened!

....

- You were born to love.
- You *are* love.
- You are *loved*!

Acknowledgements

Shane, the serendipity of our meeting was an awakening unto itself, and I have no doubt that this book would never have come to fruition if not for you. Perhaps we made a pact to cross paths somewhere along the line, or maybe this was the inevitable result of two Piscean, INFP counsellors colliding! Either way, I offer you my heartfelt gratitude for our marathon conversations, your support, love, and input as gained through your own spiritual path.

I would also like to extend my sincere thanks to Grant and Kymberley Fehon of *The Best Little Bookshop in Town* for encouraging me to do all in my power to get this out into the world. If not for bumping into you and our subsequent conversations, this manuscript would never have seen the light of day. You were pivotal in its actualisation, more than you realise. I can't thank you enough.

I thank my counselling colleagues who serve non-stop and showed an interest in what I was doing instead of presuming me to be mad. Susanne Weiley, you also helped to make this book so. (Geez, with all of these serendipitous helpers, anyone would think there was divine intervention at play!)

I also thank the seraphim of the Blue Angel team: Toni Salerno, Leela Williams, Christian Salerno, Stephanie Finn, Marie DelBalso and Tanya Graham. Thank you for physically getting this book into the world. Immense thanks are also due to Miriam Cannel.

Enormous love to my family — I picked a good one! And love to all my friends.

Last but not least, I bow down to the great energy behind All That Is. I've got one word for you, and that's *LOVE.*

....

About the Author

Lana Penrose is a former record company promotions manager, music journalist, television producer and pop star assistant. Her previous books include the bestselling *To Hellas and Back, Kickstart My Heart, Addicted to Love* and *The Happiness Quest.*

In between writing, meditating and working as a professional counsellor, Lana can often be found gazing into space. She has finally manifested a cat!

www.aguidetospirit.com
www.lanapenrose.com.au

Praise for To Hellas and Back

Travel vicariously through Lana Penrose. —Vogue

You'll laugh 'til you cry. —Cleo

Served up with generous lashings of comedy and wit. —That's Life

A hilarious and memorable read. —Famous

Lana tells us how she copes (or not) with humour and honesty. — Woman's Day

A heart-warming tale through love, loneliness, and a big fat Greek wedding to boot. —She Said

Breaks down the 'code of silence' regarding overseas experiences. — TNT Magazine, London

A story for today. —The Sydney Morning Herald

A classic fish-out-of-water, cross-cultural love story with all the trimmings. — Melbourne Herald Sun

Has all the trappings of an enthralling summer read. —Sydney Telegraph/Melbourne Herald Sun

An eventual coming to terms with differentness, a dawning of self-realisation. — Weekend Australian

Anyone who has experienced going from vibrant to dependant will empathise with Penrose. —Sunday Herald Sun

In a word: Escapist. —Weekend Gold Coast Bulletin

Hilarious and tragic. A joy to read. Thoroughly recommended. —Mount Barker Courier

Praise for Kickstart My Heart

Well-written and very personal. The kinda chick we would want to be friends with! —She Said

Welcome to the world of modern man — where women plead for pain, seek out seduction, and fall for failures. How are we supposed to tell Mr. Right from Mr. Right Now? Author Lana Penrose is hoping to give you some answers. —InPress Magazine

Having read both books, I feel as though I am now living vicariously through Lana Penrose. She has led an interesting life, and although we have never met in person, I feel as though I know her as intimately as I know my friends. —Australian Women

Prone to dating disasters? Wait till you clap your eyes on Kickstart My Heart. Madcap Hijinx. —Famous

A slew of deal-breaking experiences. —The Sydney Morning Herald

Like her first novel, this is a great read — a cautionary tale for anyone looking for romance. —TNT Magazine, London

Read while listening to its soundtrack! —Cosmopolitan

Praise for The Happiness Quest

Sprinkled with poignant details ... and laugh-out-loud humour, Penrose's story manages to convey the inner turmoil of a person suffering from depression while offering readers hope that she will find a reprieve. The Happiness Quest is an invaluable resource. Five stars. —Books & Publishing Magazine

Hilarious, insightful, and helpful, The Happiness Quest *is a great tool for anyone suffering with or trying to understand depression.* —Celia Pacquola, comedian and actor, Offspring, Utopia and Laid

Also available from Blue Angel Publishing

Crystal Stars 11.11
Crystalline Activations with the Stellar Light Codes
Alana Fairchild
Artwork by Jane Marin

The star light within your heart will lead you to sacred fulfilment for the spiritual benefit of all.

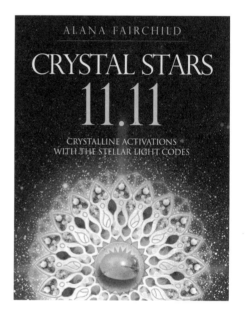

This book is for star seeds, old souls, lightworkers, visionaries, healers and hearts who hold a curiosity for the stars. This unique and powerful approach to crystal healing connects you with loving stellar beings and the precious stones that embody and enhance their transformational energy. Alana grounds the teachings with relevant and practical examples and the healing processes help you harness the therapeutic potential of each stone and form a bond with the stars so you can receive their wisdom and blessings.

Aligned with the 11.11 frequency, these celestial guides will help you shift personal paradigms and make rapid spiritual progress. Discover the healing and belonging that only comes from experiencing unity with the stars and the earth. Connect with Sirius, Andromeda, Alcyone in the Pleiades, Vega, Arcturus and other as you delve into treasured spiritual lessons on authenticity, soul passion, dark initiations, the cosmic priestess, supreme spiritual protection and more.

Beloved, you have illuminating sacred work to accomplish for yourself and the planet. Prepare yourself for the next stage of your journey with teachings and tools to help you shine like the star being you truly are.

....

Comprehensive and easy to reference with 18 full-colour crystal mandalas by soul artist Jane Marin.

Alana Fairchild is the creator of books, oracle decks, music albums, guided meditations, training programs and more. She is a bestselling author who teaches and mentors internationally. Her titles include *Kuan Yin Oracle*, *Sacred Rebels Oracle*, *Earth Warriors Oracle*, *Sacred Rebels Oracle* and the *Kuan Yin Transmission™*. Alana's creations are designed to bring out the beauty and truth of your divine inner nature so you can know freedom, courage, happiness and peace.

ISBN: 978-1-925538-76-2
Paperback, 328 pages

Also available in the Crystal Spirituality Series from Alana Fairchild:
Crystal Masters 333, Crystal Angels 444 and Crystal Goddesses 888

....

Hafiz: Wisdom of Madness
Selected Poems
Translated by Rassouli

Described as a literary wonder and a poet for poets, Hafiz has been lauded by Emerson, Goethe, Brahms and Nietzsche. Now, renowned artist and writer, Rassouli has dived heart first into the *Divan of Hafiz* to offer you fresh, careful and devoted translations so you can take your own journey into the *Wisdom of Madness*. The treasures of Hafiz will bless the reader for a lifetime.

Includes artwork by Rassouli.
ISBN: 978-1-925538-64-9
Paperback, 204 pages.

....

Kahlil Gibran - Contemplation & Creativity Journal
Featuring words and 44 full-colour images by Kahlil Gibran

This journal is a place you can savour and honour your inner world, in its entirety. And, to be inspired to authenticity. When we have only ourselves as a witness, honesty may be assumed, but it can take practice, examination and acceptance. So, be gentle and patient as you allow genuine expression to arise and spill forth on these pages. Sketches, poetry, memories, or whatever else you gift to each leaf, do so truthfully and without the desire to understand or be understood. For, Gibran tells us that to be understood, we must limit ourselves.

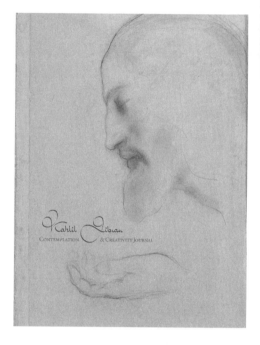

Grant yourself the freedom and delight of not being grasped, of being misunderstood. Go beyond the margins. Be limitless!

The quotes in this journal are taken from The Madman (1918) and The Forerunner (1920). Both are collections of parables and poems that prompt and goad and welcome the reader to a fresh perspective. These excerpts are presented alongside 43 full-colour artwork reproductions with thanks to the Gibran National Committee (Lebanon) and Telfair Museums (USA).

This deluxe softcover journal features 220 pages of cream-coloured premium quality wood-free paper, with a combination of lined and unlined pages to accommodate all facets of your self-expression – you may like to write, paint or sketch. Featuring quotes from Gibran's works and 44 pages of full-colour illustrations.

ISBN: 978-1-925538-78-6
220 pages. Size: 18 cm (w) x 23.5 cm (h)